War Comes to Alaska

Commemorating the Aleutian Campaign 40 years later (1982)
are Admiral James S. Russell, USN (Ret.), center; Colonel Zenji
Abe, left, who led the attack June 4, 1942; Admiral Hiroichi
Samejima, right, who led the first attack June 3, 1942.

The memorial at Dutch Harbor placed by American
and Japanese participants.

Photos Courtesy Otis W. Boise, Lt. Col.,USA (Ret.)

War Comes to Alaska

The Dutch Harbor Attack
June 3–4, 1942

BY

NORMAN EDWARD ROURKE

 Burd Street Press

This Burd Street Press publication was printed by

Beidel Printing House, Inc.
63 West Burd Street
Shippensburg, PA 17257 USA

In respect for the scholarship contained herein, the acid-free paper used in this book meets the guidelines for permanence and durability of the Committee on Production Guidelines for Book Longevity of the Council on Library Resources.

For a complete list of available publications please write

Burd Street Press, a division of
White Mane Publishing Company, Inc.
P.O. Box 152
Shippensburg, PA 17257 USA

Library of Congress Cataloging-in-Publication Data

Rourke, Norman E., 1936–
    War comes to Alaska : the Dutch Harbor Attack, June 3–4, 1942 / by Norman Edward Rourke.
        p.   cm.
    Includes bibliographical references and index.
    ISBN 1-57249-028-4 (alk. paper)
    1. World War, 1939–1945--Campaigns--Alaska--Aleutian Islands.
2. Dutch Harbor (Alaska)--History, Military. 3. Aleutian Islands
(Alaska)--History, Military. I. Title.
D769.87.A4R68 1997
940.54'28--dc21   96-53353
                                               CIP

PRINTED IN THE UNITED STATES OF AMERICA

For Connie whose love and encouragement are constant.
Here's looking at you kid!

TABLE OF CONTENTS

FOREWORD

Far to the north, where weather is a greater enemy, a small group of troops slopped through spongy tundra building a fortress to protect the American mainland. Pilots, trained to rely on accurate compass readings, found themselves using ground maps to guide their aircraft because magnetic forces skewed their instruments. Ground crews scraped, shoveled and chipped at ice, snow and frozen earth to keep planes and other equipment at the ready. Their companion air crewmen were equally stressed to fly in weather that even Arctic birds avoided. Yet they did their job, and did it well—maybe not always without some complaints. Except for the Dutch Harbor attack, the Aleutian Campaign was beset with blunders by the United States. A good example of this was sending troops to the Aleutians outfitted with tropical clothing and equipment.

The Japanese attack and ultimate invasion of the Aleutians was off limits to the press. It was initially kept a secret for morale and security reasons. Government officials and leaders feared the outbreak of panic if Americans realized how close the Japanese were to the West Coast of the Lower 48. It is no surprise, with the more expansive engagements in the South Pacific and the war in Europe, that the Aleutian Campaign is often omitted from World War II accounts.

The war in Europe and the South Pacific captured the nation's headlines as Americans followed the daily battle reports from these fronts. Yet the "Forgotten War" in the Aleutians had a significant impact on Japanese domination of the Pacific. Japan's failed attempt to divert American naval forces from Midway to the Aleutians resulted in the greatest single naval defeat for the Japanese Empire in 100 years.

In terms of great battles, heroics and historical remembrances, the Aleutian Campaign of June 1942 to August 1943 barely receives mention in history books. Likewise, June 3–4, 1942—when Dutch Harbor was attacked—is rarely noted by most historians and others who study wars. They are satisfied to analyze, write about and retell the great sea battle of Midway when the crippled United States Navy defeated a more powerful Imperial Japanese Fleet. And so it should be, for this is what America is known for: perseverance and going against the odds. Nothing should be taken from those who fought the good fight at Midway and on South Pacific battlegrounds.

In spite of this, lives were lost on both sides. And that is what makes any war important—and a tragedy.

This book focuses on the Dutch Harbor attack which opened the fourteen-month struggle in the Aleutians.

ACKNOWLEDGEMENT

Without the help of many people, former service personnel—both American and Japanese—this story would not have been told. Like most Americans, I had never heard of Dutch Harbor, and like most I was unaware of military action in Alaska. Through Ed Creamer, I learned more about this part of our American war history.

Starting with Ed's story "1183," the story of his Japanese imprisonment, I expanded my quest for more information. One of my first stops along the way was PBY crewmate Joseph R. Brown who was also a POW (though not in the same camps as Ed Creamer). Joe wrote about his experiences in *We Stole To Live*, a personal account of his service and ultimate imprisonment by the Japanese.

I am particularly indebted to Ed for his willingness to share many personal memories and memorabilia. He was especially helpful in guiding me to others who could help in either translations, or by providing additional insight into this event. He has been a special friend and brother.

From here, the story began to appear. Admiral James S. Russell, USN (Ret.), commander of VP-42, was another, and most valuable, source. Admiral Russell from his home in Tacoma, Washington, took time to review the first draft of the manuscript. His valuable experience, knowledge of the Aleutian Island seas, and the events that took place June 3–4, 1942, added the right touch. He was available via long distance for consultation, suggestions and overall direction of the account. To him I offer my most crisp military salute.

Although this is an American war story, I felt obligated to have something about the attack from the Japanese point of view. For this I ultimately made contact with Captain Teruaki Kawano (Ret.) of the Military History Department, National Institute for Defense Studies, Tokyo. Thanks to Captain Kawano, I was able to locate Mr. Hideo Obata, Tokyo, who was Air Division Officer in Charge aboard the *Takao*. Captain Kawano was even more helpful in locating photographs from Japanese archives and publications that are used here. I found myself writing Captain Kawano more often than I am sure he wished. But each time I posed a question, he graciously provided an answer. Without Captain Kawano's help, my attempts at locating other Japanese officers would have failed.

My thanks to the Japanese Embassy in Washington, D.C., for referring my initial inquiry to the Military History Department, National Institute for Defense Studies.

Vice Admiral Hiroichi Samejima (Ret.), who was a torpedo bomber squadron leader in the attack, shared articles he had written for a Japanese historical publication. He later served in the Japanese Maritime Self Defense Force.

Perhaps more bothered by me than anyone was Bernard F. Cavalcante, head, Operational Archives Branch, Naval Historical Center, Washington, D.C. Regularly bombarded with my questions and requests for information Mr. Cavalcante graciously responded in a most thorough manner.

I could not offer my thanks to those who helped without giving a big hand to three wonderfully capable librarian/researchers. Theresa Fowler, Pat Gross and Linda Reif of the Tulsa City-County Library, Broken Arrow South Branch, have shared not only in the research of this work, but in others yet to come. These three terrific women are the best at finding all sorts of books and references; even the most obscure. They are what make libraries important, exciting and the best value for taxpayer dollars.

Others who have shared their thoughts, help and support include Captain Diane J. Diekman, USN, now stationed in Japan, who gave me a priceless list of names and addresses of Navy contacts in Washington and other places; Cora Holmes, Chernofski Sheep Ranch, Unalaska, who provided names of some of the men who visited her place after the war; Annemarie McElroy, Unalaska/ Dutch Harbor Convention & Visitors Bureau, who sent more information than I could absorb in a month; Roger Mott, volunteer, at the Emil Buehler Naval Aviation Library, Pensacola, Florida, and Chuck Mai, public relations director, Oklahoma Automobile Association, Tulsa, for giving me a detailed map of Alaska—and without my being a member of AAA!

Among those who offered additional leads, personal papers and files were: Colonel C. V. Glines, USAF (Ret.), Dallas, Texas; Lieutenant General H. A. Hatch, USMC (Ret.), Vienna, Virginia; Major Rodney N. Marsh, USA (Ret.), Trapper Creek, Alaska; Lawrence Reineke, Middletown, New York; and Otis W. Boise. There are many others I am sure to have overlooked. They know who they are, and to them I offer my sincere appreciation.

My special thanks to all the men who responded to a request for information on Dutch Harbor in the *Retired Officer Magazine.* They flooded my mailbox with their stories, additional contacts, and their enthusiasm at knowing their experiences would be shared. No matter if they were a dogface in a foxhole freezing in the Aleutians, or a submarine officer patrolling offshore, each made a valuable contribution. My humble thanks to them all.

Editing drafts fell to my wife Connie. As one who enjoys a story well told, her insistence that the manuscript be error free and clear was unsurpassed. Her help and suggestions have made the difference. My thanks also to Harold Collier and Martin Gordon of White Mane Publishing for their advice and help in making this book a reality.

I take full responsibility for this work. Any mistakes are mine, and not those of these wonderful folks who served and shared their stories, talents and encouragement.

Finally, a warm thanks to Tabitha, our black feline, for reminding me what sunbeams are for on cold winter days.

Norman Edward Rourke
Broken Arrow, Oklahoma
November 1994

"I am thinking of Alaska. In an air war, if we were unprepared Japan could take it away from us, first by dominating the sky and creeping up the Aleutians. It could work both ways, of course. We could jump off from Alaska and reduce Tokyo to powder. But if we were asleep, without planes, Japan might well seize enough of Alaska to creep down the western coast of Canada. Then we would be in for it."

GENERAL WILLIAM "BILLY" MITCHELL, 1923

"Use of Alaska could shorten the Great Circle Route between the United States and the Orient—both for the United States and for an attacker. [It is] important that money be allocated to build bases in Alaska."

ANTHONY DIMOND
Alaska delegate to the U.S. House of Representatives, 1934

"Alaska is the keystone of the Pacific arch. An aerial campaign against Japan can be pushed to the best advantage from the territory. Japan is our dangerous enemy in the Pacific. They won't attack Panama. They will come right here to Alaska. Alaska is the most central place in the world for aircraft and that is true either of Europe, Asia or North America. I believe in the future, he who holds Alaska will hold the world, and I think it is the most important strategic place in the world."

GENERAL WILLIAM "BILLY" MITCHELL
Congressional hearing, 1935

"You may have thought that the Chiefs of Staff in Washington were not paying enough attention to the threat against Alaska and the Coast. We realized, of course, that such a Japanese threat could become serious if it was unopposed. But we knew also that Japan did not have the naval and air power to carry the threat into effect without greater resources and a longer time to carry it out. Preparations to throw the Japanese from that toehold, that very skimpy toehold, had been laid even before the Japs got there, and the rest of the story you know."

PRESIDENT FRANKLIN DELANO ROOSEVELT, 1944

"The Aleutians theatre of the Pacific war might well be called the Theater of Military Frustration . . . None of the operations accomplished anything of great importance or had any appreciable effort on the outcome of the war. Sailors, soldiers, and aviators alike regarded an assignment to this region of almost perpetual mist and snow as little better than penal servitude. Both sides would have done well to have left the Aleutians to the Aleuts for the course of the war."

SAMUEL ELIOT MORRISON
Aleutians, Gilberts and Marshalls, June 1942–April 1944;
History of United States Naval Operations in World War II, 1984

CHAPTER I

Keystone of the Pacific Arch

Expanding their hunting grounds, they crossed a long forgotten land bridge more than 15,000 years ago. Nomadic tribes of hunters and gatherers migrated to the land that would later be known as Alaska. It is believed by some anthropologists these nomads crossed land connecting Siberia with the Seward Peninsula. This crossing was later covered during the most recent Ice Age.

These first Alaskans developed into three groups—Aleuts, Eskimos and Indians. The Aleuts (pronounced Ally-oots) settled on the chain of islands now known as the Aleutians (pronounced Aloo-shuns). The smallest of the three groups, they were a hardy people who lived off the sea. Their food, clothing, shelter, heat and tools came from creatures living in the ocean or along its shoreline. Exceptional sailors, the Aleuts frequently paddled hundreds of miles in skin-covered canoes, called *baidarkas,* to trade, visit or stage daring raids on enemy villages.

For centuries only the native Aleuts have been able to survive in this barren land. The 1,200-mile chain of 120 stepping stone islands stretches from the Alaska Peninsula to within shouting distance of Russia's Kamchatka Peninsula. The Aleutian Chain is part of the "Ring of Fire" surrounding the outermost area of the Pacific Rim where volcanic activity is frequent.

Deep water surrounding the islands, and warm currents from the Japan Sea, keep the ports free of ice in the winter. These favorable conditions would play an important role in the future.

1

The easternmost island, Unimak, is also the largest. It measures 65 by 22 miles. To the southwest is Unalaska, where Dutch Harbor is located on the north coast. Unalaska is about 2,000 miles from San Francisco and Honolulu. Westward in order lie Umnak, Atka and Adak. Kiska is 610 miles west of Dutch Harbor. Attu, the westernmost island, is almost 1,000 miles from the Alaska mainland, and 750 miles northeast of the northernmost of the Japanese Kurile Islands. Attu is approximately 20 by 35 miles in size. Two islands—Kiska and Attu—would play a major role in the Aleutian Campaign.

Weather—its ferocity—is perhaps the most notable thing about the Aleutians. Meteorological conditions worsen at the western end of the chain. Weather is highly localized and areas of high visibility will often be found within twenty miles of fog banks.

Most notable are the sudden winds hazardous to sea and air navigation. Called "williwaws," these winds come crashing down from the mountains, sometimes reaching gale force within thirty minutes. The mountains are concentrated on the north sides of the islands. Williwaws causing strong off-shore winds make it difficult to find protection along the northern coasts. Columns of spray and mist resulting from williwaws often resemble huge waterfalls.

Weather in this region moves from west to east. As a result, the Japanese have always known in advance the prevailing conditions in the islands. This would prove valuable to them as they planned their Dutch Harbor attack.

During the early decades of the 1900s, a distant federal government was preoccupied with a war in Europe, and a depression at home. When America declared war on Japan in 1941, the nation took notice of Alaska's strategic geographical position.

Unalaska Island's most distinctive feature is Makushin Volcano. The 80-square-mile island has an elevation of 6,680 feet at the top of the volcano. The Port of Dutch Harbor, which would become a major Japanese target, is part of the City of Unalaska.

The economic base of Unalaska/Dutch Harbor is commercial fishing. Almost half the people in the community are directly involved, and more than ninety percent of the jobs depend on commercial fishing in some way. The Port of Dutch Harbor is a busy commercial fishing port. It serves more than 600 vessels including trawlers, long-liners, crab boats, cargo ships, floating factory processors and occasional cruise ships. Millions of pounds of fish and seafood are processed annually on the island.

Located 850 air miles from Anchorage, Dutch Harbor was a key coaling station and supply point for naval vessels of the Bering

Sea fleet and for whalers and sealers. During the Klondike and Nome gold rushes, the area was a major stopover for shipping to and from Seattle and St. Michales near the mouth of the Yukon River.

After 1900, Dutch Harbor almost became a ghost town. Its one claim was that it had the only brick building in the Aleutians. According to a traditional story, a Dutch ship was the first to use its harbor—thus the name. Russians called the place Udokta. In the 1890s, Americans called it Lincoln Harbor.

In 1902, the U.S. Navy became interested in Dutch Harbor. A presidential executive order set aside twenty-three acres for use as a coaling station. This plan never developed. Later in 1911, the Navy established a radio communications station on Umnak Island.

A small naval base was established at Kiska in 1916. But the project was abandoned after only a few dock pilings were driven.

Land was set aside for a wireless station at Dutch Harbor in 1912, but no military installation was built. A 1921 report on government coaling stations observed that the Aleutian Chain was practically without defense and warned that stores there "would be subject to captivity by enemy raids." The guns of World War I were silent, and the Aleutian installations went unguarded. The nation was enjoying a feeling of well-being, and disarmament treaties were popular.

In 1934 and 1935, the Navy, working with the hydrographic office, established a sun station on Kiska and surveyed some of the Aleutian Islands by air. In the process, Japanese ships were observed making soundings and charting passes and harbors. Atka Islanders reported being visited by Japanese map makers. The Navy suggested to the State Department that if foreigners were going to continue to scout these waters in the name of fish and wildlife research, an observer should be placed aboard their ships. This was not acceptable to the Japanese and so the State Department let the matter lie, dismissing Navy concerns as paranoia.

In 1922, the United States and Japan had reached an agreement in which Japan would not build bases in its newly acquired region of Micronesia. The U.S. agreed not to fortify the Aleutians or any Pacific islands west of Hawaii. But that all changed in the 1930s when Japan began a policy of expansion in eastern Asia by invading Manchuria, which was then part of China. In 1935, Japan shut off Micronesia to outsiders. Many thought the islands were being fortified.

Even though that agreement expired in 1936, the United States did nothing about the Pacific defenses beyond Hawaii until 1938. That year, Congress directed the U.S. Navy to appoint a board of officers to investigate the need for additional bases in the Pacific. Chairman Rear Admiral A. J. Hepburn recommended establishing seaplane and submarine bases at Dutch Harbor, Kodiak, Midway and Wake islands. He also recommended that the Navy build patrol plane bases at Sitka and Oahu. In 1939, Congress approved his recommendations.

The Navy established an aerology station at Dutch Harbor in July 1939. In October 1940, a Navy medical unit, and a detachment of the Marine Defense Force—four officers and 101 enlisted men—arrived. They occupied a new 125-man barracks. By early 1941, only 46 Marines remained with the mission to guard the naval installations. They did this with machine guns and four 155mm guns. In the village of Unalaska, across Iliuliuk Bay, the U.S. Coast Guard manned a station consisting of a 60-man bunkhouse, an administration building, one small seaplane hangar and shops.

The civilian firm of Siems Drake Puget Sound began building naval facilities at Dutch Harbor in July 1940. Since the U.S. Army was assigned the mission of defending naval installations, it was decided the contractor would build Army facilities also. The naval section base was commissioned at Dutch Harbor in January 1941, and the naval station in September of that year.

Troops began arriving May 8, 1941 on Amaknak Island, a small island in Unalaska Bay where Dutch Harbor is located. Until barracks were completed, soldiers lived in the Marine barracks. Most of the original marine detachment had left Unalaska by this time. The village of Unalaska on the main island had 50 whites and 250 Aleuts. On September 10, 1941, the army post was named Fort Mears in honor of Colonel Frederick J. Mears who was instrumental in surveying and building the Alaska Railroad earlier in the century.

On June 3, 1942, the Japanese attacked Dutch Harbor.

The attack brought into focus the vulnerability of the North American continent. More than 140,000 military personnel were stationed in Alaska at the time of the attack. The Aleutian Campaign—often referred to as "The Thousand-Mile War," or the "Forgotten War"—was the first battle fought on American soil since the Civil War.

For some observers, the Aleutian Campaign was viewed as a mixture of courage, brilliance, bungling, and lack of resources. Fletcher Pratt wrote in the November 1944 issue of *Harper's*:

> A good case of the stupidity is the fact that throughout Alaska territory the people for nearly two years of war never got a magazine or a newspaper from which all reference to Alaska had not been carefully clipped; and that correspondents were not allowed to mention the presence of our troops at Amchitka and

Adak until they had been there for six months, with Jap bombers coming over almost daily and telling the world about it all the time in radio broadcasts; and that even private mail was censored. A good case of the bungling was sending men specially trained in desert warfare to fight a campaign on Attu. A good case of the resource was the escape of Lieutenant Rodebaugh's PBY; and of the brilliance, the singular operations of the Blair Packing Company—but these are part of the main line of the story, and that story can be built up only against its own background.

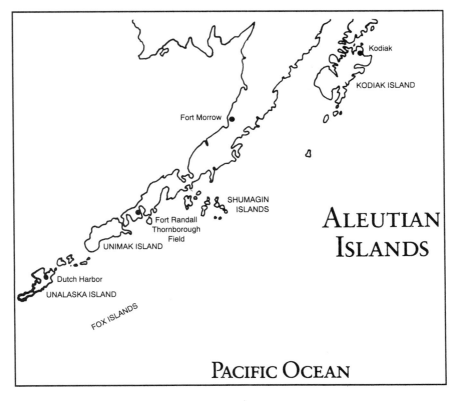

Courtesy Pictorial Histories Publishing Co., Inc.
Missoula, Mont. & Anchorage, and Chapter 103, Air Force Assn.

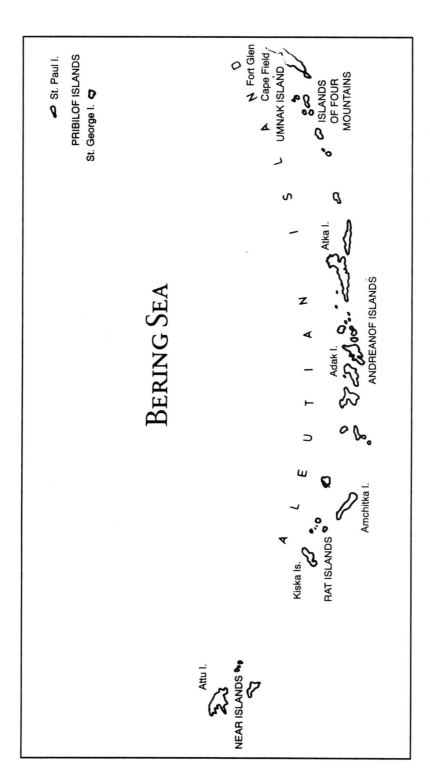

BERING SEA

St. Paul I.

PRIBILOF ISLANDS

St. George I.

Fort Glen
Cape Field

UMNAK ISLAND

ISLANDS
OF FOUR
MOUNTAINS

A L E U T I A N   I S

Atka I.

ANDREANOF ISLANDS

Adak I.

Amchitka I.

Kiska Is.

RAT ISLANDS

Attu I.

NEAR ISLANDS

Courtesy Pictorial Histories Publishing Co., Inc.
Missoula, Mont. & Anchorage, and Chapter 103, Air Force Assn.

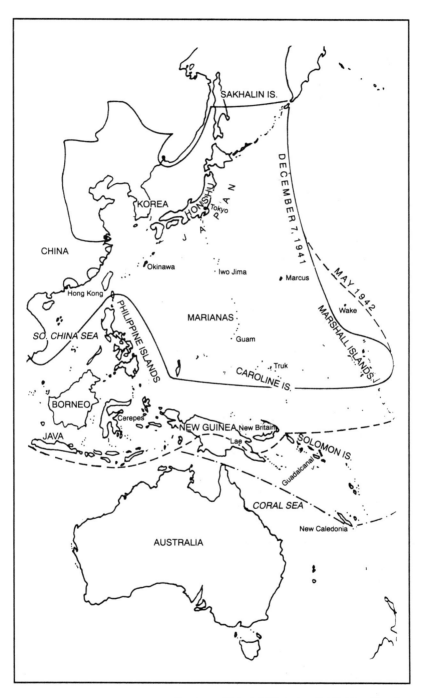

SAKHALIN IS.

CHINA

KOREA

HONSHU

Tokyo

JAPAN

DECEMBER 7, 1941

MAY 1942

Okinawa

Iwo Jima

Marcus

Wake

Hong Kong

PHILIPPINE ISLANDS

SO. CHINA SEA

MARIANAS

Guam

MARSHALL ISLANDS

Truk

CAROLINE IS.

BORNEO

Cerepes

NEW GUINEA

New Britain

JAVA

Lae

SOLOMON IS.

Guadalcanal

CORAL SEA

New Caledonia

AUSTRALIA

Courtesy Pictorial Histories Publishing Co., Inc.
Missoula, Mont. & Anchorage, and Chapter 103, Air Force Assn.

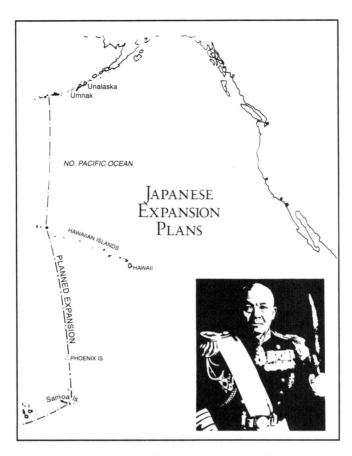

Unalaska
Umnak

NO. PACIFIC OCEAN

JAPANESE
EXPANSION
PLANS

HAWAIIAN ISLANDS
HAWAII

PLANNED EXPANSION

PHOENIX IS.

Samoa Is.

*Courtesy Pictorial Histories Publishing Co., Inc.
Missoula, Mont. & Anchorage, and Chapter 103, Air Force Assn.*

Vice Admiral Chuichi Nagumo, direct, gregarious, sentimental and uncomplicated was the instrument of Japan's bid to obtain dominance in the Pacific. Between December 7, 1941, until the Battle of Midway, his Carrier Strike Force operated across 120 degrees of longitude from the Hawaiian Islands to Ceylon in the Indian Ocean. It conducted strikes against ships and shore installations at Pearl Harbor, Rabaul, Ambon, Darwin, Tjilatjap, Colombo and Trincomalee and emerged victorious from every naval engagement. Allied losses included five battleships, two carriers, one cruiser, one aircraft tender and eight destroyers sunk or very heavily damaged; three battleships, one carrier, three cruisers and one destroyer damaged; and thousands of tons of auxiliaries and merchant ships sunk. Additionally, the allies lost hundreds of aircraft and suffered the damage and loss of docks, hangars and base facilities. Until the Battle of the Coral Sea, not one of Admiral Nagumo's ships was sunk or damaged. It was a remarkable display of naval power, unequalled in modern warfare; made even more so by the fact that Admiral Nagumo was not fitted by background, training and experience for waging carrier warfare. He had been brought up in the traditions of the battleship and the one decisive naval surface battle to which the aircraft was only an auxiliary. When confronted for the first time with the management of a major carrier battle against a foe on equal terms. Admiral Nagumo failed to grasp the complexities of naval warfare. After Midway, he lost favor. He committed suicide July 6, 1944, while commanding the ground defenses on Saipan. He was one of Japan's most formidable and courageous leaders.

CHAPTER II

Operation AL

Since the Pearl Harbor attack, Japanese forces had taken an increasing number of the Pacific islands. The Empire was anxious to lay claim to even more island territory as it sought to extend its control in the Pacific. Elsewhere, the Japanese navy scored success in the Coral Sea, and was looking toward Ceylon in the Indian Ocean as its next objective. The air war had garnered rewards even beyond the Imperial Navy's imagination in spite of some hesitancy on the part of Japanese military and political leaders. An early proponent of naval air power, Admiral Isoroku Yamamoto was pleased with the results of his aviators. Their flying skills in the latest advanced fighter, the Zero, was adding to the successes. In six months, Japanese warriors had bombed Pearl Harbor, and triumphed over Guam, Indochina, Thailand, Wake, Hong Kong; and occupied Manila, Singapore and Malaya. Along the way, the British ships *Repulse* and *Prince of Wales* had been sunk. Elsewhere in the Indian Ocean, Vice Admiral Chuichi Nagumo was adding to Japan's war treasures. Crushing Colombo along with two British cruisers, the carrier *Hermes* was also sent to the bottom.

By March 1942, the Allies had lost Java and Burma. Japanese fighting men were in the New Guinea mountains, and the Australian coast was in sight. The British had been forced out of the Indian and Pacific oceans. At Pearl Harbor, all American ships inboard of, or land-front were sunk. The U.S. Navy in the Pacific was barely afloat except for the five first class aircraft carriers that were not at Pearl Harbor. Japan had lost nothing more than a destroyer.

By May, Corregidor surrendered, then the Philippines were overcome. The Solomons, Southeast Asia and the South Pacific islands soon became Japanese territories.

The Allies were backed up to Australia from where General Douglas MacArthur was staging a counterattack. Japan's capture of as much of the South Pacific as possible was an important link in keeping the U.S.—and others—out. Control of the Pacific by Japan would include capturing Port Moresby on New Guinea's southern coast—just a fast sail from Australia.

Japan's vision of its territorial rights in the Pacific were being realized. Its concern about Russia's position, and possible involvement on the side of the Allies, only emphasized the importance of its supremacy in the Pacific. On the islands, and in the colonies, Japan could build bases from which it could hold the region and protect its homeland.

Yamamoto was convinced that if a swift strike was not made, the balance of military power would shift within two years. By striking first, the U.S. would be forced to consider terms. So strong was his belief in this that he confided to Rear Admiral Tamon Yamaguchi if the U.S. Pacific Fleet were destroyed at Midway, he would insist that Japan's political leaders initiate overtures for peace.

Yamamoto's plan was to establish a new forward defense line running from the Aleutians through Midway, Wake, the Marshalls, Gilberts and the southern Solomons. Thus it was important that the remaining U.S. naval force be drawn into a major, and final, battle that would remove that threat from Japan's Pacific conquest plan. The key would be Midway.

To assure success, naval aviation—in spite of its infancy—would play a major role. Some Japanese leaders, both military and civilian, were not so sure about the use and success of naval aviation. But Yamamoto's plan included a combined naval battle involving superiority in ships and aircraft.

The idea of a Midway attack was first mentioned in February 1942 when Japan was completing its "First Phase" of conquests. There were two lines of thinking about what should be Japan's next move: one was to move west to Ceylon, ultimately linking with German Field Marshal Erwin Rommel. The other was that Japan should go south isolating Australia, taking New Caledonia, Samoa and Fiji.

Combined Fleet commanders recommended the Midway plan for early June. It included a diversionary attack and invasion of the western Aleutian Islands. The New Caledonia-Samoa-Fiji campaign should be held off until the Midway-Aleutian plan was complete.

Such a recommendation by Yamamoto's Combined Fleet set up another confrontation between it and the Naval General Staff.

In early April discussions about Midway had begun in earnest. Commander Yasumasa Watanabe represented Combined Fleet, and Commander Tatsukichi Miyo, First Section Air Officer, represented the Naval General Staff. Miyo pleaded strongly against Midway. Citing the difficulty of gathering huge amounts of supplies, and the tactical aspects, he questioned the strategic value of Midway if the plan was successful in occupying the small atoll. He outlined the Naval General Staff's objections in a six-point document. In it he defended the alternative plan for an attack of New Caledonia, Fiji and Samoa.

His main point was that although these islands were farther away from Japan than Midway, they were about equally distant from the United States' main Hawaii base. This would nullify the U.S. defense of Midway. Finally, he argued, capturing New Caledonia, Fiji and Samoa would lower Australian and Allied morale.

While in the midst of these discussions on April 5, Commander Watanabe called Admiral Yamamoto and reported the Naval General Staff's views. He asked Yamamoto for instructions. Returning to the conference table, Commander Watanabe quoted Admiral Yamamoto's uncompromising position:

"In the last analysis, the success or failure of our entire strategy in the Pacific will be determined by whether or not we succeed in destroying the United States Fleet, more particularly its carrier task forces. The Naval General Staff advocates severing the supply line between the United States and Australia. It would seek to do this by placing certain areas under Japanese control, but the most direct and effective way to achieve this objective is to destroy the enemy's carrier forces, without which the supply line could not in any case be maintained. We believe that by launching the proposed operations against Midway, we can succeed in drawing out the enemy's carrier strength and destroying it in a decisive battle. If, on the other hand, the enemy should avoid our challenge, we shall still realize an important gain by advancing our defensive perimeter to Midway and the western Aleutians without obstruction."

With this strong statement, the Naval General Staff realized Yamamoto was not going to give up on Midway, nor was he willing to accept an alternative. Leaders of the Naval General Staff reluctantly agreed to Yamamoto's plan. Although an agreement of sorts was met, the timing of the plan continued to be one of contention between Combined Fleet and the Naval General Staff.

The latter urged postponement of N-Day (code name for the Midway invasion day) for at least three weeks. Combined Fleet pushed for early June for execution of its plan. It was essential, Combined Fleet said, that the attack be launched when the moon was full.

The Army General Staff fully agreed with Combined Fleet's plan, and was willing to cooperate without hesitation. Although not a change of heart in its feelings toward navy policies, the army quickly saw the Midway-Aleutian operation as a navy plan, while the army would provide only a small number of troops as landing force reinforcements.

******

April 18, 1942: Japanese Prime Minister Hideki Tojo left for a routine inspection trip. Nearing the port of Mito, a strange aircraft was sighted. The Prime Minister's plane veered sharply to avoid a mid-air collision with the on-coming bombers. Sixteen brown U.S. Army Air Force B-25s commanded by Lieutenant Colonel James Doolittle were on their way to Tokyo and other inland cities of Japan. Although damage was slight, the raids shook Japan's confidence in its isolated security. As a result of the Doolittle raids, opponents to Yamamoto's Midway-Aleutian plan were quick to cease their argument. Many thought the raiders had come from Alaska since Doolittle was from there. (Other Japanese leaders believed Doolittle's raid was launched from Midway.) Little did they know that far out to sea on the heaving USS *Hornet,* the raiders chanced a carrier-launched bomber attack.

******

On May 5, 1942, Navy Order 18 was issued:

By command of His Imperial Majesty to Commander in Chief Yamamoto of the Combined Fleet:

1. The Commander in Chief of the Combined Fleet is to cooperate with the army in the occupation of Midway and strategic points in the west of the Aleutians.

2. Detailed directions will be given by the chief of the Naval General Staff.

Twenty days later, May 25, 1942, aboard his flagship the recently built battleship *Yamoto,* Admiral Yamamoto hosted a gathering of 200 officers. The occasion was to celebrate the sailing of the greatest armada Japan had ever put to sea. Its goal was to draw the crippled U.S. naval force from Hawaii and finish the job that was begun with the attack on Pearl Harbor. Although Yamamoto was anxious to carry out his plan, he had no misgivings about the fighting will of the United States. After studying at Harvard, he became a Japanese naval attaché in Washington. He traveled the country extensively and perhaps knew more about his American foes than his fellow officers.

******

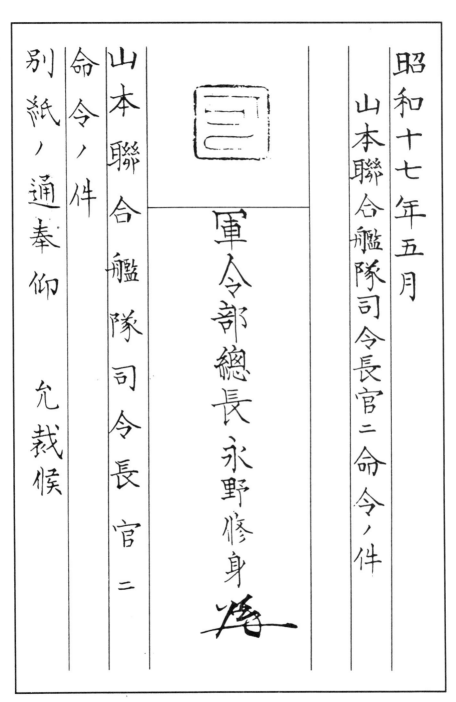

昭和十七年五月
山本聯合艦隊司令長官ニ命令ノ件

軍令部總長 永野修身

山本聯合艦隊司令長官ニ
命令ノ件
別紙ノ通奉仰 允裁候

This is Navy Order 18 from Emporer. Japanese reads left to right.

指示セシム

大海令第十八號

昭和十七年五月五日

奉勅　軍令部總長　永野修身

山本聯合艦隊司令長官ニ命令

一、聯合艦隊司令長官ハ陸軍ト協力シ「ミッ
ドウエイ」島及「アリューシャン」群島西部要地
ヲ攻略スベシ

二、細項ニ關シテハ軍令部總長ヲシテ之ヲ

Operation AL—the Japanese code for the Aleutian Island campaign—would begin with an initial attack on Dutch Harbor—the largest base in the Aleutians. Information on the harbor had come from Japanese submarines that had reconnoitered the area. In the original plan following the attack, the islands of Attu, Kiska and Adak would be invaded. (The invasion of Adak was later cancelled.) The Aleutian invasion force was to be withdrawn by mid-September to avoid the harsh winter. Some Japanese historians have said the Aleutian Campaign was never considered to be a prelude to an invasion of the United States mainland. Rather, its goal was to disrupt the supply line between the United States and the USSR, and protect Japan from Alaska based air attacks. The invasion would also put the United States on the alert that its western shores and defense plants in Washington were vulnerable.

For the Japanese naval commanders, the Aleutian attack was to be a diversion from the main effort against Midway. American leaders perceived the Aleutian Campaign as part of a major effort to control the Pacific from north to south. Japanese naval leaders expected part of the paltry American Pacific Fleet to be diverted to the Aleutians, thus weakening even more the defenses at Midway. At the same time, by pulling some of the American ships northward, a successful naval battle, in which Japan would have superior firepower in both areas, would result in crushing the American Pacific Fleet once and for all.

Walter Lord, author of *Incredible Victory*, a book about the Battle of Midway, published in 1967, said the Aleutian Campaign was not a diversion to draw the American Pacific Fleet from Midway.

According to Lord, Commander Tsunoda, "a resident expert on Midway" at the Japanese War History Office, told him the Aleutian phase of the Midway plan was part of the on-going feud between the Combined Fleet and the War Plans Section of the Naval General Staff. Admiral Osami Nagano, chief of the Naval General Staff, overruled his own War Plans Section in favor of Yamamoto's Midway plan, according to Tsunoda.

Yamamoto, according to Lord, quickly agreed to the Aleutian phase as presented by the War Plans Section as a way of allowing them to save face. The War Plans Section preferred an Aleutian campaign—including the capture of Attu and Kiska—as a safety measure against U.S. air attacks from the north. They wanted it to take place at the same time as the Midway attack.

Japanese war games held during the Ceylon campaign involved sham attacks on Tokyo by Aleutian-based U.S. aircraft. This strengthened the idea of taking the Aleutians.

Later during his research, Lord again posed the diversion theory to Commander Tsunoda. Lord stressed that all previous accounts called the Aleutian campaign a diversion. Commander Tsunoda repeatedly said the Japanese fleet was strong enough at the time to make a diversion unnecessary. He also stressed again the real reasons for including the Aleutians were those he had presented earlier, e.g., a feud between the Combined Fleet and the Naval General Staff.

Regardless of whether the Aleutian Campaign was a diversion or not, for fourteen months a unrecognized war would be waged in the unforgiving climate in this harsh land. The capture by the Japanese of Attu and Kiska would be the first American territory held by a foreign power since 1912.

Organization of Japanese Forces for the Occupation of the
Western Aleutians
June 1, 1942

Commander in Chief Combined Fleet—
Admiral Isoroku Yamamoto

Northern Force, Commander in Chief Fifth Fleet—Vice Admiral Boshiro Hosogaya; Chief of Staff, Captain Tasuku Nakazawa:
  Nachi, flagship, Captain Takahiko Kiyota, heavy cruiser.
  2nd Section, Destroyer Division 21: 2 destroyers.

Second Mobile Force, Commander Carrier Division 4—Rear Admiral Kakuji Kakuta:
  Carrier Division 4:
    Ryujo, flagship, Captain Tadao Kato.
    Junyo, Captain Geito Ishii
  Second Section, Cruiser Division 4:
    Takao, Maya
  Destroyer Division 7:
    Ushio, Oboro, Akebono
  Oiler, *Teiyo Maru* (later named the *Toho Maru*)

Adak-Attu Occupation Force, Commander 1st Destroyer Squadron— Rear Admiral Sentaro Omori; Chief of Staff, Commander Rokuji Arichika.
  1st Destroyer Squadron, less 3 divisions:
  Abukuma, flagship, light cruiser.
  Destroyer Division 21:
    Wakaba, Hatsushimo, Nenobi, Hatsubaru.
    Kinugasa Maru with Army North Seas detachment embarked
      (301st Independent Infantry Battalion, Major Masatoshi
      Hosumi, commanding. Approximately 1,200 men).

Magane Maru, mine layer.

Kiska Occupation Force, Commanding Officer of Kiso—Captain Takeji Ohno.
> 21st Cruiser Division:
> > *Kiso, Tama.*
> 22nd Cruiser Division (less two auxiliary cruisers):
> > *Asaka Maru*, converted light cruiser.
> Destroyers:
> > 3 from 27th Division, two from 6th Division:
> > *Hakusan Maru*, with No. 3 Maizuru Special Naval Landing Force embarked with approximately 550 men, Lieutenant Commander Mifumi Mukai, landing force commander.
> > *Kumagawa Maru*, with 700 labor troops embarked.
> > *Kaiho Maru, Shunkotsu Maru, Hakuho Maru*, gunboats.
> > Subchaser Division 13: 7 of 8 subchasers

Submarine Force, Commander 1st Submarine Squadron:
> 1st Submarine Squadron: *I-9*, flagship.
> > Submarine Division 4: *I-25, I-26*; Submarine Division 2: *I-15, I-15, I-19*: 5 submarines

Seaplane Force:
> *Kimikawa Maru* and attached float planes: 1 seaplane carrier, 14 float planes, 1 destroyer.
> Escort: *Shiokaze.*
Base Air Force, Commanding Officer of Flying Boat Unit—Captain Sukemitsu Ito:
> Detachment of Toko Naval Air Group: 6 flying boats.
> *Kamitsu Maru, No. 2 Hino Maru, No. 2 Hishi Maru, No. 5 Seiju Maru*, cargo ships.

Attached Forces:
> *Awata Maru*: converted cruiser.
> *Fujisan Maru*: oiler.
> *Teiyo Maru*: oiler.
> *Nissan Maru* (oil, gasoline, coal): collier-oiler.
> *Akashisan Maru* (miscellaneous auxiliary stores and munitions): cargo ship.
> *No. 2 Toko Maru* (stores ship).
> *Muroto*: cargo ship.

Added subsequently during June 1942:

    To 2nd Mobile Force:

        Aircraft carriers: *Zuikaku* (June 20) and *Zuiho* (June 9)

        Destroyer Division 4 (June 9): 4 destroyers.

    To Submarine Force (June 9):

        2nd Submarine Squadron:

            Submarine Division 7: *I-1, I-2, I-3.*

            Submarine Division 8: *I-4, I-5, I-6.*

    To Seaplane Force (June 9):

        Kamikawa Maru and attached float planes: 1 seaplane carrier; 14 float planes.

        Escort: *Hokaze*, destroyer.

Source: *The Campaigns of the Pacific War*. United States Stategic Bombing Survey (Pacific) Naval Analysis Division, 1946.

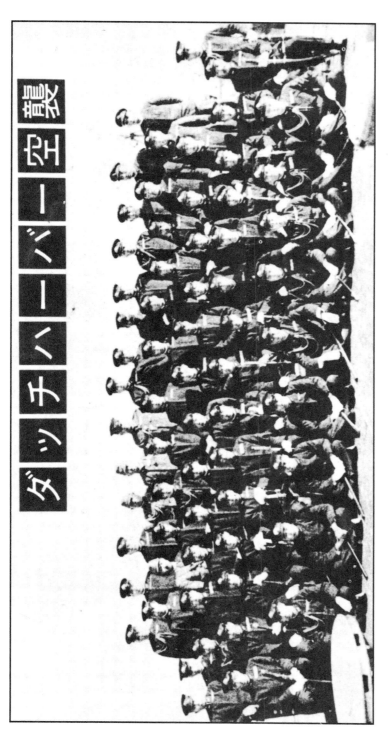

ダッチハーバー空襲

Aboard the Japanese carrier *Nachi*, May 25, 1942, at the Ominato Naval Base. Key officers in the photo are in the second row: seventh from the left is Rear Admiral Kakuji Kakuda, commander of the 4th Aviation Squadron; eighth from the left is Vice Admiral Boshiro Hosogaya, commander of the 5th Fleet; ninth from the left is Rear Admiral Sentaro Omori, commander of the 1st Destroyer Squadron.

Courtesy Maru Magazine

20

昭和17年6月5日、龍驤より出撃した攻撃隊はダッチハーバーを攻撃し、飛行機格納庫を炎上させる戦果をあげた。写真は爆撃後、帰途につく龍驤の九七式艦攻である。この日の対空砲火は激しく護衛の零戦隊のうち古賀1飛曹の機が不時着、のちに米軍が回収してテスト飛行を行なった。写真の機体は主翼下面に大きく62と書かれているが、このようなマーキングは珍しい

Japanese Kate returning to home carrier *Ryujo* after the attack June 4, 1942.

Courtesy Maru *Magazine*

The 2nd Strike Force sorties for the Aleutian attack May 26, 1942. To the left are the *Hakusan Maru* and the *Kimigasa Maru*. On the right are the carriers *Ryujo* and *Junyo*.

Courtesy Maru *Magazine*

Unidentified Japanese carrier.
Courtesy Maru *Magazine*

Admiral Isoroku Yamamoto, commander in chief of the combined fleet.
Courtesy of U.S. Naval Historical Center

22

EXTRA

Anchorage Daily Times

HEART OF ALASKA'S FAIRWEATHER

EXTRA

TWENTY-SIXTH YEAR   ANCHORAGE, ALASKA, WEDNESDAY, JUNE 3, 1942   PRICE TEN CENTS

RAID DUTCH HARBOR!

WASHINGTON, D.C., June 3. (AP)---The navy announced today that four Japanese bombers and about 15 fighters attacked Dutch Harbor at approximately 6 o'clock this morning.

The attack lasted 15 minutes, the communique said. No other details were available at this time.

The Navy announced that the Dutch Harbor attack caused no serious damage. There were only a few casualties.

The second communique based on reports received to 6 p. m., eastern time, said "further reports on the Japanese air attack at Dutch Harbor state there were but few casualties. A few warehouses were set afire but no serious damage was suffered. There is nothing to report from other areas."

BLACKOUT TONIGHT

400 Planes Hit Essen In New Raid

Promise Nazis 30,000 Planes Every Month

British Score New Successes On Desert, Canterbury Bombed

By Associated Press

Great Britain's desert army lashed out today in an offensive 30-mile thrust against the axis in North Africa while RAF bombers perhaps one strong battered German war formations in the driven stricken city of Essen for the second time in 24 hours.

Huge fires were left burning in the city of 660,000 population.

In London a spokesman told the objectives of the raid assaults on Cologne in the Ruhr valley were already substantially achieved and de clared that the boast that 30,000 RAF planes would bomb Germany each month was "not fantastic."

London military headquarters acknowledged that axis troops mopped up on flexible futures on a nine-mile sector along a 30 mile British defense line but the British air supply lines were seriously endangered by a thrust at Rotunda Segnali. This major axis base is 30 miles west of the advanced axis positions.

Front line dispatches said the Germans were now established at the new alignment after withdrawing westward. A violent tank battle was reported in progress at Knightsbridge, 25 miles southwest of Tobruk.

The RAF blasted Canterbury, German night raiders attacked Canterbury, commandoes said, in-the-German planes tingley started at Fourth avenue...

"Weeping Women of Kerch" Bemoan Dead

On the battlefields of Russia weeping women of Kerch area eat their dead slain and left in piles by Germans as Russian snipers who drove Wehrmacht from the locality look on with sympathy. Original photo arrived in New York from Russia as Germans stepped up offensive on Eastern Crimea and Russians gained near Kharkov.

Police Chase, Arrest Man

Catch Wild Driver After Tipsy Ride

After what city police officers described as a wild drive through town at better than 30 miles an hour, Lloyd Mattox, Jr. was jailed at 2:30 o'clock this morning, and later released on bail of $100. He was charged with reckless driving, speeding, failure to stop at stop signs and emerging from an alley at to private property.

According to officers Christian and Hansen reported that Mattox tingley started at Fourth avenue and C street, drove west to K at more than 50 miles an hour, turned south on K in the alley between Sixth and Seventh avenue and down the alley, cut...

Our New Warhawk

Figure 5. In flight for the first time is the Curtiss P-40F, or Warhawk fighter. Faster and with a higher ceiling than its predecessor, the...

Ask 8 Billion For 500 More Battleships

Chairman Vinson Will Introduce Bill For Largest Naval Program

WASHINGTON, June 3...

UMA Avoids Split With CIO

A CHICAGO ...

Chinese Cut Jap Advance

(By Associated Press)

Chinese guerrillas today reported General Chiang's armies cut a triangular chunk in the flank of the Japanese lines in the Chekiang province and in eastern Kiangsi provinces north west of Nanhai.

The report said heavy rains were bogging down the Japanese advance north of China's east front some miles along...

Six Are Dead In Navy Crash

SAN FRANCISCO, June 3.— Navy reported that six were killed 20 miles south of here near Mill Moon Bay when a navy aircraft crashed...

Call For War Against Three More Nations

City Must Be Dark As Pitch, CD Orders Say

Raid Wardens Get Patrol Instructions, Close Loop Road

At the same time, Fort Richardson authorities, announced that the Loop Road out of Anchorage is closed to civilian traffic permanently. All motorists were advised to make no attempt to use it.

Mr. Raynor declared that the blackout tonight must be absolute. Special measures were being taken to bring about an efficient enforcement of the order.

The blackout restrictions included a ban on the use of any kind of light covered with blinds or other colored paper and, no even extended to smoking in the open.

It was the most urgent blackout yet issued, Cooperation of the public with civilian defense and police officials was regarded to make it effective.

Wardens and block chiefs were being instructed and that it covers that the CD blacked regulations are reached in all houses, shops, stores and other places.

Automobiles must keep headlights dim. Street lights and illuminated signs must be extinguished.

"Homes must be dark," W. J. McDonald, in charge, declared...

23

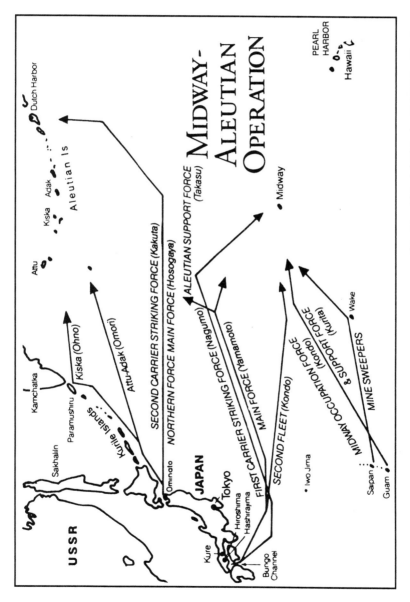

MIDWAY-ALEUTIAN OPERATION

Courtesy Pictorial Histories Publishing Co., Inc.
Missoula, Mont & Anchorage, and Chapter 103, Air Force Assn.

CHAPTER III

Enemy Contact

January 1942: Japanese submarines are seen in the area of Dutch Harbor. Three of them fire on the installation and immediately dive.

April 1942: A Japanese plane crashes in the Aleutians reportedly from wing icing. Three officers and one enlisted man are killed. Four others crawl to safety. Nothing more was heard of them.

—Unconfirmed Reports

******

Not unlike their American counterparts, the Japanese Imperial High Command debated the military strategy and significance of an Aleutian campaign. Also like his counterpart, Admiral Chester W. Nimitz, Japan's Admiral Isoroku Yamamoto, commander-in-chief of the Combined Fleet, was an early supporter of air power. It bothered him that five first-class U.S. aircraft carriers had escaped the Pearl Harbor attack. With these ships afloat, Japan's superiority of naval air power would be significantly hampered.

While his commanders planned the Midway attack, Yamamoto was bothered by the nearness of American airplanes in the Aleutians. By luring the aircraft carriers to the Aleutians for defense, Japan's bombers would have a shorter range and greater advantage over them. This would give him the balance of power in Midway.

An Aleutian attack would also cut the supply line between the United States and Russia—another bothersome enemy of Japan.

24

Perhaps more important to the Japanese, an Aleutian invasion would stop any drive by the U.S. to attack Japan from this northern territory.

(Conversely, American military strategists saw the Japanese invasion as a prelude to the invasion of North America. However, according to Japanese military leaders, this was never their goal.)

Other Japanese commanders preferred to focus their efforts on Australia. But Lieutenant Colonel James Doolittle changed all that. When his B-25 bombers raided Tokyo and other inland cities they caused only slight damage, but the raid shook Japan's sense of isolation.

This event changed Japanese military minds. They could not afford to have their homeland so vulnerable. As a diversion to Midway, they would attack Dutch Harbor, hoping to pull aircraft carriers away from the U.S. South Pacific Fleet, thus weakening any protective naval shield at Midway. Japan would succeed in smashing once and for all the presence of an American naval force in the Pacific. At the same time Japan could establish flying boat patrol bases in the Aleutians, putting them a mere twelve hours away from Seattle's Boeing plant and the Bremerton Navy Yard in Washington. It would also put them within a dagger's thrust of the supply jugular of the Soviet Union.

Rear Admiral Robert A. Theobald, commander of Task Force 8 believed, like others, the Japanese would attack Dutch Harbor, Cold Bay and Umnak Island from the air. They would follow with an invasion force to control these areas.

On May 28, 1942, Pacific Fleet Commander Admiral Chester A. Nimitz told Admiral Theobald Japanese invasion/occupation forces were poised to take the islands of Attu and Kiska (this proved to be correct). But Theobald would not accept this, and held to his original belief that Dutch Harbor, Cold Bay and Umnak Island were the Japanese targets.

As a result, Theobald kept his task force in the eastern waters of the Gulf of Alaska. He also persuaded Brigadier General Simon Bolivar Butler, the U.S. Army's top officer in Alaska, to transfer more than half his aircraft to Cold Bay and Otter Point. Theobald then rendezvoused with his task force 400 miles south of Kodiak.

******

1000 hours June 2, 1942. After a grueling patrol, the PBY crew had just landed on the steel mesh runway layed over the spongy tundra. While ground crews refueled the aircraft, the patrol plane's crew set to cooking their evening meal over a small gas burner: hamburgers, bread, butter, canned pears and coffee. Within minutes after eating, they huddled in four bunks and sleeping bags in the aircraft for a well deserved rest. It was quiet except for the ever rushing Aleutian wind.

0300 hours June 3, 1942. Barely three hours after settling down, an alarm was sounded. Command Pilot Lieutenant (j.g.) Jean Cusick ordered his mechanic to crank up the balking engines of the plane. The crew was soon awakened by the shuddering aircraft and noise. The PBY lifted off into the black freezing night. As the air grew colder, rain changed to sleet and then snow. Numbing air rushed through the plane's open gun hatches.

Cusick and his eight-man crew took to the dark Arctic air from their base on Umnak Island. For seven long and grueling hours, the lumbering Navy PBY 5A patrolled the skies. The plane and crew were part of PBY Squadron 41 that had been ordered to Dutch Harbor in May as part of a defense build-up in the Aleutians. Reports of a Japanese fleet kept the amphibious patrol planes busy. The patrols were a routine that had become almost mundane. On board, the crew settled into its work. Second Pilot Lieutenant (j.g.) Wylie N. Hunt sat next to Cusick.

Behind them in the twin engine gray aircraft were third pilot George Morrison, machinist/gunner Joseph Rust Brown, radiomen Jack Collins and Louis E. "Euchre" Yurek, gunner Carl E. Creamer, machinist mates Sam Davis and Burdette Siler.

0540 hours. On the seaplane tender *Gillis,* the radarman picked up a dozen blips on his screen. They were moving fast, coming in above the clouds. The planes were about 10 miles out and flying at 10,000 feet. The *Gillis* flashed a warning to the base and sounded general quarters.

Naval Station Commander William N. Updegraff wasted no words to the signalman to order air raid red alert. He ordered the six ships in the harbor to build up steam in their boilers. The air raid warning rapidly worked its way across Unalaska Island from Dutch Harbor to various outposts.

Within twenty minutes, Japanese Zeros from the carrier *Junyo* bombed and strafed Dutch Harbor. Captain Leslie E. Gehres at Kodiak Island received only fragments of information on the attack. Wasting no time, and using code, he contacted his operations officer at Dutch Harbor. With the bits and pieces of information he had, Captain Gehres believed the Japanese carriers were located north in the Bering Sea. Thus he concentrated all PBYs to search that area.

But two PBYs went southwest into the onrushing force of the *Ryujo* ("Free Flying Falcon") and its sister carrier *Junyo* ("Prancing Dragon"). One of these was Lieutenant Cusick's aircraft. Two-hundred miles from Dutch Harbor, Cusick stumbled into *Junyo*'s attacking patrol. In a split second, the swift Zero fighters blasted the slow flying PBY. In spite of evasive actions, the Navy amphibious plane was no match for the likes of Japan's finest fighter aircraft. In short order, the PBY crashed into the freezing waters. Five crewmen survived the attack and ditching. While they struggled to keep alive on life rafts, the cold water and injuries took their toll. Cusick and Morrison did not make it.

After six hours in the Bering Sea, the Japanese heavy cruiser *Takao,* steaming out of the mist, saw the three survivors. They were hauled aboard. For them the war was over as they spent the remainder of it in various Japanese prison camps.

(About their being picked up by the *Takao,* Creamer said: "The Japanese cruiser passed us by the first time. The weather and high seas made it dangerous to stop and pick us up. But evidently the ship's skipper was told to pick us up for questioning. The second time the ship nearly missed us.")

On the following day, several hundred miles south, one of the greatest naval battles in history would take place at a Pacific atoll known as Midway. That battle would bring the war to the 1,200-mile string of Aleutian Islands. But what happened in the Aleutians would not garner the notoriety of the Battle of Midway.

Back home on the American mainland, families of the ill fated PBY that was shot down while patrolling the stormy Bering Sea and North Pacific waters would learn the fate of their loved ones. The pain and anticipation for the next three years would be as much had these men been part of the more famous sea battle.

******

LIEUTENANT (JUNIOR GRADE) JEAN CLARE CUSICK
U.S. NAVY, ACTIVE, DECEASED

"Officially reported to be MISSING IN ACTION as of 3 June 1942, when the plane in which he was flying, a unit of Patrol Squadron FORTY-ONE, was shot down while in contact with the enemy off Dutch Harbor, Alaska . . ."

******

Lieutenant (j.g.) Wylie M. Hunt's report as recorded in USSBS Interrogation Nav #118, pg. 534 and following:
Our takeoff time was 0300 on June 3, course approximately 210ø, ground speed about 130 knots; heavy overcast, squalls and light rain. We flew until about 0500 at which time we were attacked by Japanese fighter planes covering a carrier of an attacking force. We were searching by radar and had had no indication of the enemy's presence before the attack. Our starboard engine was shot out in the first attack and our plane set on fire. We were flying at about 1,000 feet, [it was] overcast at about 1,500 feet. Several fighters

made one pass apiece at us. Our course was approximately down wind, but a turn was made and we landed into the wind. The pilot Lt (j.g.) Cusick received one bullet through his arm. He and the enlisted pilot [George Morrison] made the landing. As a result, immediately upon landing, the plane began to fill rapidly with water and sank a very few minutes after landing. We estimated our position to be 200 miles, bearing 210ø from Umnak Field. The plane captain and the remainder of the crew got out the large seven man life raft and attempted to launch this raft. I stopped and picked up the small two man life raft and launched it. I then assisted the first pilot away from the burning plane and into the raft. After we were aboard the raft, we saw that the crew were having trouble getting the large raft launched. In the small raft, besides Lt. (j.g.) Cusick and myself were Brown S1c, third mechanic of the plane and Creamer AOM3c, gunner.

The large raft had bullet holes in it and would not float so two more men swam over and hung on to the side of the two man raft. These men were the plane captain, Siler, and the enlisted pilot Morrison. Siler stayed with our raft for a few minutes and then, seeing the large raft still afloat, swam back to it and tried once again to make it seaworthy. He was unable to do so and as we were drifting quite rapidly with the high wind, he was unable to reach us again. Morrison remained holding to the side of the raft for approximately one hour before he died of exposure. Lt. (j.g.) Cusick died from his wound and the cold about one hour after Morrison.

The three of us left in the raft drifted for approximately five hours more until about noon, at which time we were sighted by a Japanese cruiser [*Takao*] operating with the attacking force. It steamed over and picked us up. The cruiser which picked us up, I recognized as a heavy cruiser with five turrets. The three of us were in pretty bad shape at the time we were picked up due to the cold. Brown was almost unconscious. The Japs threw a line down, which Creamer secured around Brown's waist and the latter was hauled up to the deck of the cruiser by the Japanese crew. Creamer and I made our own way up a steel ladder which they lowered to us. I was able to get up the ladder until my waist was even with the deck and then couldn't get any further. As soon as we were aboard ship, we were given a hot bath. Our clothing was removed and kept and we were dressed in Japanese clothing. We were then taken below deck.

******

HIDEO OBATA, AIR DIVISION OFFICER IN CHARGE, *TAKAO*

My questions and his [one of the survivors of the downed PBY] answers were as follows:

Q: Did you have any information in advance, concerning the approach of the Japanese task fleet?

A: No, I don't know.

Q: Where is the base of the P-40 wing?

A: I don't know.

He repeatedly insisted that he had been given no information relating to the questions in the briefing given prior to his departure. Then I decided to finish the questioning and had a chat with him. He told me about his sweetheart, showing her picture. He knew of the prisoner camp in Zentsuji too.

He was a graduate from the Naval Reserve Officers Training Course.

His attitude was fine. He proudly said that he had accomplished well his duty for his motherland states. He was an excellent officer.

ORGANIZATION OF UNITED STATES FORCES IN THE NORTH PACIFIC

JUNE 1, 1942

North Pacific Force, Commander Task Force Eight—Rear Admiral Robert A. Theobald.

Nashville, flagship, heavy cruiser.

Air Search Group, Commander Patrol Wing 4—Captain Leslie E. Gehres

20 amphibian flying boats, 4 heavy cruisers, 3 small seaplane tenders.

Surface Search Group, Commander Alaskan Sector—Captain Ralph C. Parker

One gunboat, 1 mine sweeper, 5 Coast Guard cutters, 14 small patrol vessels.

Air Striking Group, Commanding General, 11th Army Air Force—Brigadier General Simon Bolivar Buckner, Jr.

Three Army fighter suadrons, 1 Army heavy bomber squadron, 1 Army medium bomber squadron, 1 Army composite group, 1 Navy fighter squadron, 1 Canadian Reconnaissance squadron.

Destroyer Striking Group—Commander Wyatt Craig

7 destroyers.

Submarine Group—Commander Lake

6 submarines.

Main Body—Rear Admiral Robert A. Theobald

2 heavy cruisers, 3 light cruisers, 4 destroyers.

Tanker Group—Commander Maples

2 oilers.

Source: *The Campaigns of the Pacific War.* United States Strategic Bombing Survey (Pacific) Naval Analysis Division, 1946.

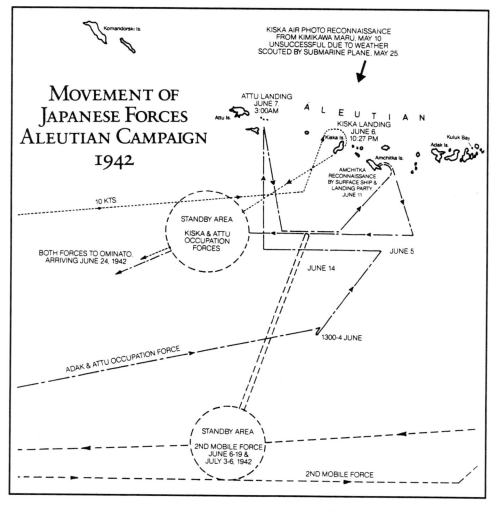

Komandorski Is.

KISKA AIR PHOTO RECONNAISSANCE
FROM KIMIKAWA MARU, MAY 10
UNSUCCESSFUL DUE TO WEATHER
SCOUTED BY SUBMARINE PLANE, MAY 25.

Movement of Japanese Forces Aleutian Campaign 1942

ATTU LANDING
JUNE 7,
3:00AM

Attu Is.

A L E U T I A N

KISKA LANDING
JUNE 6,
10:27 PM

Kiska Is.

Kuluk Bay

Adak Is.

Amchitka Is.

AMCHITKA
RECONNAISSANCE
BY SURFACE SHIP &
LANDING PARTY
JUNE 11

10 KTS.

STANDBY AREA
KISKA & ATTU
OCCUPATION
FORCES

BOTH FORCES TO OMINATO,
ARRIVING JUNE 24, 1942

JUNE 5

JUNE 14

1300-4 JUNE

ADAK & ATTU OCCUPATION FORCE

STANDBY AREA
2ND MOBILE FORCE
JUNE 6-19 &
JULY 3-6, 1942

2ND MOBILE FORCE

Courtesy Pictorial Histories Publishing Co., Inc.,
Missoula, Mont. & Anchorage, and Chapter 103, Air Force Assn.

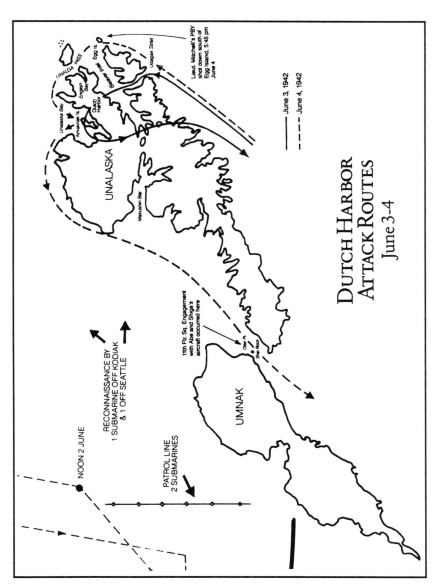

DUTCH HARBOR
ATTACK ROUTES
June 3-4

UNALGA PASS

Unalaska Bay
Erskine Bay
Dutch Harbor
Amaknak Is.
Beaver Inlet
Egg Is.
Ulagaan Strait

Lieut. Mitchell's PBY
shot down south of
Egg Island, 5:45 pm
June 4

UNALASKA

Makushin Bay

————— June 3, 1942
– – – – June 4, 1942

UMNAK

11th Ftr. Sq. Engagement
with Abe and Shiga's
aircraft occurred here

Otter Pt.
Ship Rock

RECONNAISSANCE BY
1 SUBMARINE OFF KODIAK
& 1 OFF SEATTLE

NOON 2 JUNE

PATROL LINE
2 SUBMARINES

Courtesy Pictorial Histories Publishing Co., Inc., Missoula,
Mont. & Anchorage, and Chapter 103, Air Force Assn.

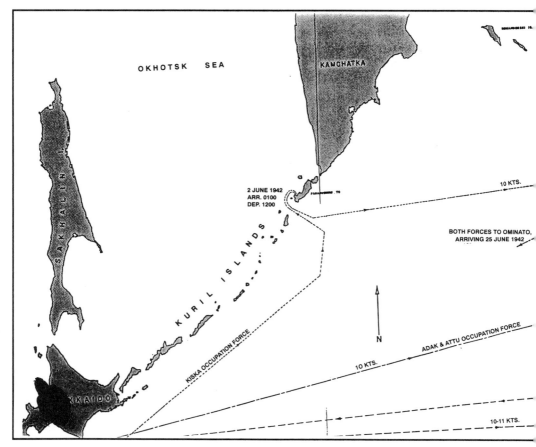

U.S. Navy and Japanese navy track charts show the Japanese
naval attack force movements in the North Pacific
leading up to the Dutch Harbor attack.

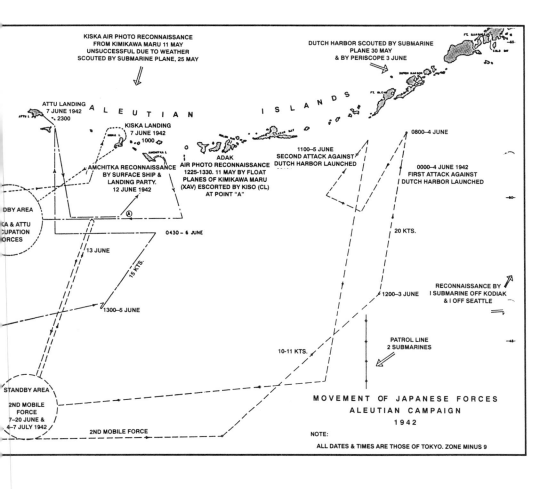

KISKA AIR PHOTO RECONNAISSANCE
FROM KIMIKAWA MARU 11 MAY
UNSUCCESSFUL DUE TO WEATHER
SCOUTED BY SUBMARINE PLANE, 25 MAY

DUTCH HARBOR SCOUTED BY SUBMARINE
PLANE 30 MAY
& BY PERISCOPE 3 JUNE

A L E U T I A N   I S L A N D S

ATTU LANDING
7 JUNE 1942
2300

KISKA LANDING
7 JUNE 1942
1000

0800—4 JUNE

AMCHITKA RECONNAISSANCE
BY SURFACE SHIP &
LANDING PARTY.
12 JUNE 1942

ADAK
AIR PHOTO RECONNAISSANCE
1225-1330. 11 MAY BY FLOAT
PLANES OF KIMIKAWA MARU
(XAV) ESCORTED BY KISO (CL)
AT POINT "A"

1100—5 JUNE
SECOND ATTACK AGAINST
DUTCH HARBOR LAUNCHED

0000—4 JUNE 1942
FIRST ATTACK AGAINST
DUTCH HARBOR LAUNCHED

DBY AREA

KA & ATTU
CUPATION
ORCES

Ⓐ

0430 – 6 JUNE

20 KTS.

13 JUNE

15 KTS.

1300—5 JUNE

1200—3 JUNE

RECONNAISSANCE BY
I SUBMARINE OFF KODIAK
& I OFF SEATTLE

PATROL LINE
2 SUBMARINES

10-11 KTS.

STANDBY AREA

2ND MOBILE
FORCE
7–20 JUNE &
4–7 JULY 1942

2ND MOBILE FORCE

MOVEMENT OF JAPANESE FORCES
ALEUTIAN CAMPAIGN
1942

NOTE:

ALL DATES & TIMES ARE THOSE OF TOKYO. ZONE MINUS 9

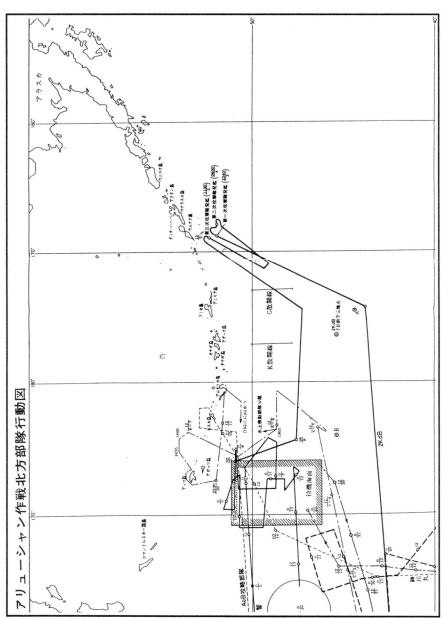

CHAPTER IV

Attack

Submarine and air bases are being built in eastern Siberia in a joint German-Russian project. These bases are located on Big Diomede Island, just three miles from Alaska's Little Diomede Island—U.S. news wire report.

******

It was later learned the Russians were building a weather station.

In late May 1942, Japanese scout submarines reconnoitered the western Aleutian Islands, Dutch Harbor, Kodiak and Seattle for ship concentrations. American forces were ordered to maximum alert from May 30 through June 4. All leaves were cancelled, and ammunition was issued. On Dutch Harbor, a full alert was in force with around-the-clock aircraft patrols. Reveille was moved from 0300, battle stations were manned from 0430 to 0600. If no attack occurred by 0600, normal security routines took effect.

Many American military leaders believed the Aleutians would be stepping stones for a Japanese invasion of the North American continent. Ironically, the Japanese saw the Aleutians as a jumping off spot for an American invasion of their island empire.

Communications problems compounded the Aleutian defense. The Army and Air Force operated on different radio frequencies, and both were different than the Navy's! In addition, the radios each service used were not balanced. They were scrounged from various sources, and oral—slow phonetics—communication was the only way messages could be sent and received.

35

Out to the west of Dutch Harbor, on Umnak Island, an Army secret base—Fort Glenn—was established. There, twelve P-40s were based. The Japanese did not know of Fort Glenn, or of the P-40s.

******

Aleutian weather is unforgiving to both friend or foe. The storminess of the region takes its toll on those who are protecting democracy as well as those who would destroy it. Thus it was for the Japanese fleet headed toward the Aleutians. Ironically, far to the south in the Pacific, as Admiral Yamamoto's fleet was closing in on Midway, it suffered similar stormy weather. The only difference would be the temperature of the water where flyers would crash their fighters. To the north, Japanese pilots would face not only the flak and shore batteries, they would have to play a close game of chance with the surging sea. If they dipped too close while following the drift of the waves to get their bearings, they would soon be in the water.

June 3: Aboard the Japanese aircraft carrier *Ryujo* squadron leader Lieutenant Masayuki Yamagami knew his mission would not be easy. A squall was blowing in. The hard driving rain was cold, the sea more choppy and uninviting than ever. Soon he and the 17 planes in his squadron took off from the surging deck of the carrier. Airborne, the 11 Type 97 Kate attack bombers and six Zero fighters quickly got into formation. After Lieutenant Yamagami's squadron was airborne, Lieutenant Hiroichi Samejima's Zero left the flight deck in command of another squadron.

The temperature at sea level was 0 degrees centigrade. Reports from a Japanese scout submarine said the weather was clearing near Unalaska and Dutch Harbor. The attackers flew low to avoid the thickening fog.

Just after takeoff, Samejima noticed his air speed decreasing. Slowly throttling more power, he realized his carburetor was freezing. Around him his squadron was falling behind. He thought they were having the same problem. Should he turn back or stay on course for the attack?

If he continued, he might be forced to ditch his plane in the stormy sea. He would surely die if he did so. The throttle was almost wide open as the plane's engine struggled to overcome the cold air rushing through it. Suddenly the engine roared to full power! The carburetor icing had finally cleared. Samejima throttled back, smoothing out the engine. The new squadron commander drew a deep breath of comfort, knowing he could carry out his duty.

Lieutenant Commander Norman F. Garton, *Gillis* captain, was alerted to the incoming attack planes. He signaled the base and sounded general quarters.

In the harbor were destroyers *King* and *Talbot,* a submarine and a Coast Guard cutter. The ships weighed anchor and stood ready with all hands at battle stations. Ashore the naval air station had been at general quarters since 0430.

Since June 1, a 24-hour alert was in force from Nome to Seattle. Aircraft were on patrol as far as their fuel would endure. Patrol pilots relied heavily on radar, looking for enemy planes and ships. Radar was also important in preventing the planes from smashing into fog-shrouded mountains. There were too few aircraft not to be careful.

During a patrol on June 2, the *Ryujo* and *Junyo* were discovered less than 400 miles south of Kiska. As a defensive move, more Army Air Force planes were ferried to airfields at Cold Bay and Umnak Island.

Ten minutes into his mission, fate favored Lieutenant Yamagami and his squadron. The eye of the storm passed over, allowing him to set his sights on Dutch Harbor. Below, U. S. Navy personnel took aim, peppering the sky with flak and ground fire. Other battery commanders sighted the attacking planes and started shooting at them. For Lieutenant Yamagami and his pilots, the flak was intense and nerve wracking. But they kept their target in sight and carried out the attack.

By 0555 sixteen bombs released by the first flight of torpedo bombing planes had fallen on Dutch Harbor. Two fell in the water, and 14 hit nearby Fort Mears. Although little damage was done to structures and military targets, 25 men were killed and an equal number were wounded. Destroyed were a barracks and three Quonset huts. Other buildings were also damaged.

Some of Lieutenant Samejima's squadron damaged the radio station and demolished another Quonset hut. A third flight of attackers targeted wooden oil tanks which had been there for many years. Their bombs overshot the tanks, but killed a Navy fire watcher in his pillbox and the driver of an Army truck.

Shore batteries and ships in the bay at Dutch Harbor put up a heavy barrage of fire. The naval air station commander praised the effort of the USS *President Fillmore* as it led the barrage on the attacking planes.

"In addition to her own armament, she had mounted on deck a battery of 37mm guns consigned to Cold Bay, which gave her 22 antiaircraft guns. These were served with such rapidity that the *Fillmore* appeared to be—and was reported—on fire," he said.

The *Gillis* claimed two Japanese attack planes. No naval ship was damaged during the attack.

Ten minutes after the attack began, a flight of P-40 fighters arrived from Cold Bay on Unimak Island east of Dutch Harbor. There was no one to fight. They returned to the base without firing a shot.

Turning into the squall, Lieutenant Yamagami led his pilots back to the *Ryujo* and safety. By now the weather had worsened. His squadron could not maintain formation. He ordered his pilots to break up into smaller flights and find their way back to the ship on their own. No more than 50 feet above the lapping waves, they struggled to reach the carrier. Freezing in unheated cockpits, nearly out of fuel and hoping not to ditch in the cold, stormy waters, they sighted the *Ryujo*. Happily they formed up for a bouncing, yet safe, landing on the ship's deck. The mission was over.

Lieutenant Yamagami said he was "surprised at the accuracy and how fast antiaircraft guns were in operation." This was definitely not like the Pearl Harbor attack where complete surprise was met with little or no opposition. Japanese aerial photographs taken during the June 3 attack showed Dutch Harbor was better equipped than had been imagined.

But while groping their way back to the *Ryujo*, one of the pilots passing over Makushin Bay spotted a squadron of destroyers apparently lying in wait. This was radioed ahead to Task Force Commander Rear Admiral Kakuji Kakuta. When all his planes were safely aboard (except for one that was lost over Dutch Harbor), Admiral Kakuta sat in on the pilots' debriefing. He listened intently to their description of the raid.

Shortly after Lieutenant Samejima's squadron was on its way to Dutch Harbor, Admiral Kakuta ordered another attack group to take off from the sister ship *Junyo*. Because of the wicked weather and fog, this group passed Lieutenant Samejima's squadron without either knowing it. Ironically this was that group's second attempt. On the first they got lost in the fog and had to return to the ship.

By the time the *Junyo* squadron was finally airborne and on their way to Makushin Bay, the weather had worsened. As a result they missed the ships in the bay and could not find Dutch Harbor. A Japanese-speaking American radioman intercepted their call for help to get back to their ship. He gave them directions believing he had sent them far out to sea and into the worsening storm. However, his accent did not fool the Japanese pilots. They were able to sort out the true signal from the false and were brought safely back to the carrier.

At the same time the planes from the *Junyo* were sent off, four Pete catapult-launched seaplanes were sent aloft. They came from the *Takao* and the *Maya*. They encountered even worse luck than the planes from *Junyo*. Getting off course and lost, they came out of the edge of the storm within sight of Umnak Island where a secret air base was located. Below, Private George Stanley of the 11th Fighter Squadron was washing bed sheets outside the hospital tent. It was not a particularly enjoyable job, but it was his.

The strong GI soap was notorious for cleaning just about anything, while making the user's eyes suffer. Private Stanley tilted his head back to clear his eyes. Doing so he spotted four enemy planes circling overhead. Responding quickly, he sounded the alarm and calmly returned to his laundry duty.

This time the American fighters were more successful. Twenty-one P-40s scrambled aloft. The Japanese seaplane pilots did not see them until it was too late. The Americans chased one seaplane and shot it down to the cheers of GIs on the ground. One of the remaining three planes was driven out, riddled with machine gun bullets and crashed into the sea. The other two escaped safely and returned to their ships. During debriefing, the Japanese pilots could not say where the American planes came from. The secret Umnak base remained secret.

The first attack on Dutch Harbor was over.

June 4: American airmen on patrol came upon the Japanese naval force—the Second Mobile Force. Navy PBYs and B-26 Marauder bombers attacked the ships in an effort to destroy them, or at least damage them sufficiently to lessen their threat. But for all their enthusiasm and determination, the attacking U.S. planes did little or no damage. Using all their resolve in dive bombing, the PBYs and B-26s did not seriously disrupt the Japanese attack plan.

Meanwhile, to the south, Admiral Yamamoto was having his own problems. The U.S. Pacific Fleet successfully avoided his submarine screen and was closing in. When Admiral Kakuta's attack planes were halfway to Dutch Harbor for the second day's attack, Yamamoto sent a sharp message to his Aleutian invasion force commanders: they were to postpone the invasion of Kiska and Attu, and head south at full speed to join Yamamoto's reserve north of Midway.

It was too late. The Japanese attackers were well on their way to Dutch Harbor again, and Kakuta could not bring them back. Admiral Kakuta had more important things on his mind right now. He would join his naval comrades to the south as soon as he had carried out the Dutch Harbor attack and safely recovered his planes and crews.

Prior to the June 4 attack, incoming B-26 bombers were fired on by jumpy ground gunners. Fortunately none of the Marauders were hit. The bombers would be part of the counterattacking force now that the Japanese ships were located.

The weather in the morning had been as unpleasant as it had the day before. In spite of the poor visibility, PBY surveillance of the Japanese ships continued. One of the Navy scout planes was damaged by antiaircraft fire from a Japanese ship. Later in the day the weather improved, offering a clear evening and scatter clouds.

1740 June 4, 1942, Fisherman's Point Army Observation Post: Three flights of Japanese dive bombers were reported headed for Dutch Harbor. They were reported near Mt. Ballyhoo. (The name was given by Jack London during a stay at Dutch Harbor, the locale of *The Sea Wolf*.) At 1800, ground gunners opened fire on the Japanese attackers. Ten fighters, flying in a low strafing attack, struck the naval air station. Following these, 11 bombers, using openings in the overcast, made dive bombing attacks. Each of the bombers was armed with one heavy bomb released in a low dive at 1,500 to 1,000 feet.

Four new fuel oil tanks which had been filled for the first time on June 1 were destroyed. They contained 22,000 barrels of fuel. An adjacent diesel oil tank was punctured and caught fire. Bunkers around the tank held the burning oil, preventing it from reaching the rest of the fuel tank farm.

The *Northwestern,* an old Alaska coastal ship being used for a contractors' barracks, was partially destroyed and set afire by the attackers. Fast working crews flooded the engine room and saved her. Months later, the defiant ship's engines were used to provide power, steam and heat to the island community.

Japanese attackers also scored hits on a warehouse and a hangar housing a PBY-5A.

1821: Three horizontal bombers approach Dutch Harbor from the northeast. Their five bombs fall harmlessly in the harbor. At 1825, the last attack of the day came. Five planes approaching at high altitudes from the northwest drop bombs near the magazine area on the south slope of Mt. Ballyhoo. Nine of the bombs do nothing. But the tenth kills an officer and three men in a Navy 20mm gun emplacement. Japanese fighters also strafed shore installations at Fort Glenn on Umnak Island.

Total American casualties for the two days were 33 Army, eight Navy, one Marine and one civilian killed and about 50 wounded.

Counterattacking PBYs and B-26s dive bombed the Japanese ships at sea. One B-26 went into a sharp dive attempting to arm the torpedo it carried. Water impellers on the torpedoes were the normal arming devices used when the weapons were released in the water.

A PBY flown by Lieutenant Charles E. Perkins was armed with a torpedo and two 500 pound bombs. Perkins spotted the Japanese task force and radioed his position: "Going in to attack . . ." He was about to launch his torpedo on the *Junyo* when his right engine took a direct hit. Jettisoning the torpedo and bombs, Perkins limped back to the base on one engine.

Aboard the *Ryujo*, Air Officer Masatake Okumiya watched in horror as a B-26 released its torpedo like a bomb. Heaving seas tossed the ship up and down in heavy swells, causing part of its deck to be flooded with tons of water before the ship surged to the top of another swell. As the torpedo sped amidships, the carrier fell into a trough before being thrust on the crest of another wave. The weapon zipped across the ship's deck harmlessly.

Commenting on the Dutch Harbor attacks and invasion of Attu and Kiska, Hideo Obata, who served as air division officer aboard the *Takao* said, "While the Japanese succeeded in the campaign [Dutch Harbor attack], I was sorry that I lost two scout seaplanes under my command. In spite of our success, I anticipated that it would be difficult to control the air and sea surrounding the western Aleutian Islands because the local weather condition was so bad, and those islands were far distant from our home bases in Japan. It would be very difficult to secure our sea lines of communications, to deploy and maintain adequate forces there, and to accomplish effective and offensive operations. Mere occupation of some islands has little strategic significance. The Japanese failure in the Midway campaign made [my concerns about the Aleutians] more probable or certain."

The two-day attack was witnessed, and experienced by several Army, Navy and Air Force personnel and one civilian. Their stories give personal insight into the opening attack of an oft forgotten part of World War II history.

ART BAUMAN, PHOTOGRAPHER, USN

As a Navy photographer, Bauman flew with the pilots in patrol bombers, taking photographs of the Aleutian terrain. His photos helped decide where air strips would be built. They also identified Japanese installations, ships and submarines. After his Dutch Harbor stint, Bauman served in Algeria, France, Italy, Sicily, and other battlefronts. Bauman took more than 3,000 photographs during his four-year military service.

"I saw a Navy PBY mail carrier heading out of the harbor for a run to Kodiak. Japanese fighters came in low and attacked the plane. It was just taking off when a Zero came in shooting. It [the PBY] landed on a spit of land and burst into flames. It was a gruesome thing to see.

"At Dutch, we were told an attack was coming, but no one knew when. When the Japanese finally arrived, we did a lot of praying. If you've ever heard of 'foxhole conversions', there were a lot of those during the attack. I think when people are in a dangerous spot, when man alone can't help, they do call out for divine protection. I was one of them.

"I felt secure, although I would be lying if I didn't say I was scared. Everyone was fearful. As you saw the bombs coming down in strings, you felt pretty helpless. I was as scared as anybody.

"They said there was no way off the island so it was every man for himself. Dig your foxhole and get in it. In fact most of us slept in a foxhole waiting for things to happen. I spent two nights in a foot of water. I kept my down sleeping bag on.

"More planes were lost [in Aleutian service] because of weather than in combat. There were very few clear days. Pilots routinely got lost because the radar, which was in its infancy, would easily go out. When your are in the fog, you can fly five or six hours and barely see the wing tips. The pilot would have to rely on his knowledge of the islands."

S/SGT. HARREL CHANCELLOR, CO. I, 3RD BTLN., 137TH INF.,
WEAPONS PLATOON SERGEANT

"My outfit arrived at Dutch Harbor about midnight on June 2. We were quartered in a barracks about a half mile inland from 'Navy town' on the harbor. I got my platoon up at 3:30 the next morning [June 3] to go to the dock to unload our equipment. The Japanese attacked at daylight while we were aboard the USS *President Fillmore*. Japanese planes were bombing and strafing Fort Mears and the Naval Air Station for about two or three hours. I saw one fighter plane cripple the PBY mail plane as it was taking off across the harbor.

"I worked my platoon back to our barracks at Fort Mears after taking cover under the Navy theater for 30 minutes. We took cover in foxholes and hillsides near our barracks. The enemy planes were bombing Fort Mears. They hit just about every other building. Luckily my barracks was skipped, but the engineering barracks on one side, and the officer's club on the other were struck. We had a lot of dead and injured. My platoon was covered in their foxholes. I lost only one man who was cut by shrapnel. He was not deep enough in the hole.

"The bombing and strafing attack caused quite a lot of damage. The Japanese didn't seem to have any specific targets. They hit barracks, warehouses, oil storage tanks, planes on the ground, ships in the harbor and ammunition dumps.

"We had a few hours of calm, but they attacked us again the next evening [June 4]. This attack was much the same as the day before with one exception. Most of the troops had dispersed from the Fort Mears area to the hills and shoreline at Captain's Bay where they dug in. Some of the enemy fighter planes strafed the hills and shoreline.

"My company was dug in on Hill 400, where I had machine guns on the rim at a 50-foot cliff. One made two passes by our position, spraying sand over myself and four of my men. We waited for more attacks, but none came."

CPL. BERT TRIEMSTRA, 155MM FIELD ARTILLERY GUNNER

"Our field artillery unit arrived in Seattle headed for Guadalcanal. The troop ship was loaded with 155mm artillery pieces, and all the uniforms needed for the jungles in the South Pacific.

"As we were walking up the gang plank, news came that Central Intelligence decoded a Japanese message which said they were headed on a two-pronged attack. One task force was headed for Midway, and the other was headed to Dutch Harbor.

"We were actually supposed to go west of Dutch Harbor and out-maneuver the Japanese, making a landing before they did. But we hit a terrific storm on the way and one of our buddies got thrown out of his upper bunk and broke his arm. Dutch Harbor had the last hospital in the Aleutians. While in the harbor, we received a report that unfriendly planes were approaching, and it wasn't long before Japanese planes were dropping bombs all around us.

"Thank the good Lord there was a heavy fog in the harbor. They missed us completely, but bombed the daylights out of a civilian ship docked at the pier [the *Northwestern*]. In the meantime, a destroyer guided us out of the harbor. It took us to Chernofski Bay to protect us from the Zero fighters.

"Those guys [PBY crews] had a lot of guts flying in the most terrible weather in the world, and at their slow speed trying to bomb a Japanese aircraft carrier!

"The Japanese did not know the engineers had just laid down some metal strips so our P-40 fighters could take off to attack the Zeros.

"We finally waded ashore on Umnak Island west of Dutch Harbor. The PBYs kept us informed concerning the whereabouts of the Japanese carriers. The Zeros kept strafing our positions, but they were ignorant [of the recently completed airstrip], because they could have landed and taken the island. We were outnumbered. They retreated to Kiska and Attu where we finally took care of them."

LOWELL THORSNESS, CIVILIAN CATERPILLAR DRIVER WORKING WITH THE MILITARY BUILDING ROADS

"My foreman told us word was received the Japanese had sent carriers from Tokyo Bay with orders to bomb Dutch Harbor. [The Kiska and Attu Occupation Forces and Second Mobile Task Force sailed from Hokkaido.] We were told to get ready. He told us to dig a foxhole because they were coming.

"Typical of construction crews, someone said 'Let's get up a pool,' and we made bets on the day of the attack. Little did I know I'd be helping dig out bodies a few days later.

"On the second day, I was in a bomb shelter with eight other guys. Most of them were infantry firing 30-06 Springfields. One guy fired two rounds when his rifle jammed. In the middle of the bombing, he's sitting there talking to his rifle! He's telling it he had it in Fort Ord [California] and it never failed him, and he had it in the desert maneuvers and it never failed. Then he says: 'The first Jap I see you fail me...' He used some strong language."

TED JOHNSON, PBY PILOT

"I was coming down through the clouds and fog, breaking out at about 900 feet. On my right was a carrier going away from us at right angles. No airplane was in sight, so I reached up and rammed the throttles full bore on both engines. We were trying to duck back into the clouds.

"Shortly afterward, one of our engines began heating up and had to be shut down. I jettisoned the torpedoes to maintain altitude, then set my course toward Dutch Harbor.

"I flew 180 miles back and was so busy flying that plane I didn't have time to be scared. One bullet had cut the oil line.

"But that's what we were there for. Find the enemy, report their position and take your lumps. We did it all without escorts."

FREDERICK JAMES BARBERO, CEM (AA), ELECTRICIAN, USN

"Just prior to the attack on Dutch Harbor we all knew that an invasion was imminent. Our only defense was a small naval force including a division of World War I S-boat submarines. At that time I was the chief electrician's mate aboard the S-35.

"We were ordered, with the other boats, to form a north-south picket line, hoping to intercept the invasion force. Without radar, and so few covering such a large area, it was a futile attempt. The only excitement was when our lookouts spotted an 'aircraft carrier' which proved to be, after an approach, only an outcropping of rocks with a carrier's shape!

"After returning to Dutch Harbor, we learned of the attacks and were told that two warehouses, one containing boots, the other butter, were demolished. A grounded station ship [*Northwestern*] was also destroyed."

JOHN CLOE, HISTORIAN, 11TH AIR FORCE, ELMENDORF AIR BASE, ANCHORAGE

"Dutch Harbor was well prepared. Our intelligence had broken their radio and they [Navy] knew it was coming almost to the hour.

Most of the people who got killed had just gotten off ships the night before. Nobody had told them what to do.

"[When] The Japanese showed up, they [newly arrived American troops] piled out of the barracks and got hit."

JOHNNIE JENKINS, USN, MESS STEWARD

[Jenkins arrived with Army troops the day before the Dutch Harbor attack.]

"We sat around drinking that first night. The next morning [June 3] when everything happened, everyone left me because I hadn't been assigned to a duty station.

"I tried to get into a foxhole, but the guy in there told me I couldn't get in because he was from Alabama and I was Black. With the Zeros strafing us, I wasn't about to leave that foxhole, and I told him so.

"We got along fine, and he invited me back the next day, but I had made other arrangements."

WILLIAM JAMES HURST, ENSIGN, GUNNERY OFFICER

"The USS *Talbot* (DD 114), an old four stacker destroyer, was operating off the West Coast when it was directed to go into the San Francisco Shipyard to have five new 20 mm guns installed.

"As gunnery officer, I took a group of men to the firing range to get experience firing and maintaining the new weapons. Upon arrival at the range I was advised that the battleships had priority so my crew could not fire the guns. Needless to say, the battleships were not going any place where they would need the guns for a long time.

"In late May 1942, the ship departed the States for Dutch Harbor, escorting three old S-Boats. After a long, slow, rough trip we approached the Aleutian Islands. Two of the S-Boats were detached and headed to stations further out the Aleutian chain. We proceeded with the remaining sub into Akutan Pass. The strong wind against the tide made an extremely rough passage. The entire ship's forecastle would disappear in the waves and the water hit the bridge with such force we weren't sure if we could keep going. Finally we came out of the Pass into less rough waters. We waited for what seemed like ages with no sight of the sub. We feared it had been lost, so we proceeded to Dutch Harbor and went alongside a fuel dock. The facility consisted of a short dock with fueling connections and pilings to secure bow and stern lines.

"The captain reported the missing sub to the authorities ashore. Sometime later we heard the Army shore battery, located on the harbor entrance, firing. After we realized they were firing at the sub, we called the battery by signal light. After considerable difficulty getting them to understand our message, we convinced them the sub was friendly. The fact that a sub was approaching the harbor on the surface in daylight and signaling them by light didn't seem to indicate to them it might be friendly.

"The sub had submerged when it hit the rip tide and cleared the Pass at a slow submerged speed. One officer (the Executive Officer, I think) had been knocked out before submerging. Most of the structure around the periscope was ripped off.

"We were notified to be alert for some type of action, so we kept our engineering plant lighted off and ready to get under way on short notice. We continued to receive fuel by gravity flow from a hose all night. The fuel tank was only a short distance from the pier.

"The next morning I assumed the watch as officer-of-the-deck at about 0345. Later in the morning, I noticed some airplanes over the mountains at a considerable distance. With binoculars, I realized they were not friendly, so I sounded the ship's general alarm and notified the engine room to stand by to answer all bells. I notified personnel [handling] the fuel hose to cut the line holding [it] in the fuel trunk, and [for] the personnel standing by the mooring lines to the pilings to take them in.

"As soon as the captain arrived on the bridge he relieved me and I took my station as gunnery officer on the flying bridge. A person from the fuel depot came running down the pier yelling to not cut the fuel hose loose. About that time a stick of bombs hit the fuel tank area. He fell flat on the pier and then got up and left without another word.

"A plane had approached us from the harbor side strafing as it came in. The only damage received was a cut antenna. It appeared that our 20 mm guns had hit the plane as it passed close overhead. Luckily we had practiced shooting our guns at balloons almost daily on the trip north. Our gunners had become good, far better than what we saw the battleship gunner doing back at the range.

"In short time, we were under way proceeding out of the harbor. By then there were several Japanese planes attacking the shore installations. I watched Japanese fighters shoot a couple of PBYs that were trying to take off. Unfortunately our main battery of four inch guns was single purpose (for surface fire only), but the executive officer stationed at the after gun had it shoot at a plane anyway. It was only good for the morale.

"The ship proceeded to Makushin Bay, a short distance from Dutch Harbor, where we joined a few other old destroyers. We were told to be prepared to get under way to conduct a torpedo attack on the carrier group if it was located in time and within a reasonable distance. We never received the order to search for the carrier.

"When we returned to Dutch Harbor, several persons ashore said their first notice of the attack was our general alarm. The *Talbot* continued operating in the Aleutian area through the landings on Adak and Amchitka islands."

Summary of Air Effort
Japanese Attack on Dutch Harbor, June 3-4, 1942

	Japanese		U.S.	
	Available	Lost	Available	Lost
Fighters	20	1	32	2
Light Bombers	36	5	—	—
Medium Bombers	—	—	20	1
Heavy Bombers	—	—	6	1
Flying Boats	—	—	20	4
Float Planes	6	1	—	—
Total	62	7	78	8

Results at Dutch Harbor:

Casualties	43 killed, 50 wounded
Destroyed	4 oil tanks and 20,000 barrels of fuel oil, 2 barracks, 4 huts, one 20 mm gun and emplacement, one Navy flying boat (PBY-5A) destroyed on the ground.
Damaged	1 barracks ship (SS *Northwestern*), 1 warehouse, 1 hangar.

No damage to ships of the Japanese Second Mobile Force.

Source: *The Campaigns of the Pacific War*, United States Strategic Bombing Survey (Pacific) Naval Analysis Division, 1946.

AMERICA GETS A ZERO

The U.S. gained an important trophy from the Dutch Harbor attack. The famed and feared Zero was the leading war machine in the Japanese aerial arsenal. During the attack, Flight Petty Officer Tadayoshi Koga's plane was damaged by a shot through its oil line. Koga's wheels down landing in the Aleutian tundra was a fatal mistake. Upon touching the boggy ground, his wheels stuck in the muck flipping the plane over. Koga died as the result of a broken neck.

Later, American crews recovered the Zero. It was examined carefully and its features studied to learn how to combat the fearsome fighter.

In the book *Zero!*, published by Ballentine in 1956, Jiro Hirokoshi retells Air Operations Officer Masatake Okumiya's account of the Dutch Harbor attack and the lost plane:

"Early in the morning of June 4, 1942, the aircraft carriers *Ryujo* and *Junyo* of Rear Admiral Kakuji Kakuta's 2nd Carrier Task Force approached Dutch Harbor. The task force's stealthy and unobserved move to the Aleutians actually was the opening blow of the Midway and Aleutian Operations. Lashed by cold winds and driving rain, the *Junyo* launched six Zero fighters and twelve Type 99 Val dive bombers in the first attack against the American positions. Our flight formations encountered several enemy flying boats which they engaged and destroyed. This delay in flight, in addition to the violent storms encountered en route, forced the Zeros and Vals to abandon their mission.

"However, six Zeros and eleven Type 97 Kate attack bombers from the *Ryujo* failed to encounter enemy aircraft on their approach to Dutch Harbor. Led by Lieutenant Masayuki Yamagami, the formation battled heavy rain and thick fog, arriving over the enemy base above a solid layer of clouds. Fortunately the sky cleared directly over the harbor and our planes dove to the attack. The Kates bombed the radio stations and pier installations, while the Zeros escaped from enemy fighters, strafed a number of flying boats tied to harbor buoys.

After the attack the bombers and fighters reassembled over the eastern end of Unalaska Island, where Flight Petty Officer Tadayoshi Koga noticed his Zero trailed a thin spray of gasoline [this was later found to be oil from a line that had been cut by ground fire]. Informing (his leader) Kobayashi that he did not have enough fuel to return to the *Ryujo*. Koga dropped low over a small island [Akutan] eastward of Dutch Harbor, which had been designated as an emergency landing site for crippled planes. Once down on the island, the pilots would be picked up by a submarine.

"On his return to the carrier, Kobayashi reported to his superior:

'The emergency landing site appeared from the air to be flat and clear. Koga made his approach perfectly, but immediately after the wheels struck the ground, the airplane tipped over, remaining upright [actually the plane flipped over]. The Zero appeared to be heavily damaged and either the pilot died or he must have been seriously injured. Since the island surface seems to be tundra, it would be difficult to remove the wreckage. We could not discern any sign of human habitation in the vicinity.

'Koga apparently realized that to land in the water off the island would have been certain death, for the temperature was so low that only several minutes of exposure to the cold would have killed him. Notified of the emergency crash landing, our submarine scoured the area, but did not sight the wreckage on the island.'"

The impact of the loss of the Zero was expressed clearly by Okumiya:

"In the Aleutian campaign I was Admiral Kakuta's air staff officer. I could not realize at the time how far reaching an effect this seemingly trivial incident of losing to the enemy a single intact Zero could have. We felt strongly that the unnoticed capture of the airplane, assisting the enemy so greatly in producing a fighter plane intended specifically to overcome the Zero's advantages, did much to hasten our final defeat.

"Meanwhile, in Japan, our government harped on the victories of the Aleutian attacks and the island occupations. The continual emphasis on our successes in the far north was, of course, merely a diversionary effort to conceal from the people the terrible losses at Midway."

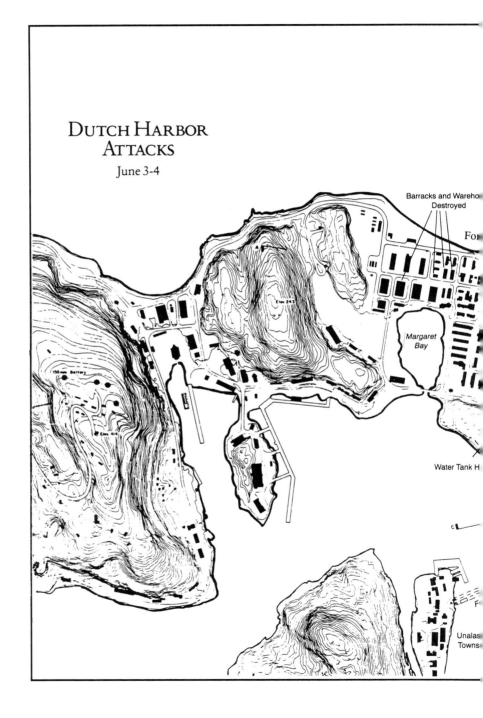

DUTCH HARBOR
ATTACKS
June 3-4

Barracks and Wareho
Destroyed

Fo

Margaret
Bay

Water Tank H

Unala
Towns

Courtesy Pictorial Histories Publishing Co., Inc.,
Missoula, Mont. & Anchorage, and Chapter 103, Air Force Assn.

SS *Northwestern* burning after being hit by a
bomb during the Dutch Harbor attack.
Courtesy National Archives

The SS *Northwestern* after the attack.
Courtesy National Archives

**U.S. Marines on alert between attacks. Smoke from burning
fuel tanks in the background was set afire by a Japanese
dive bomber the previous day.**

Courtesy National Archives

U.S. Navy machine gun crew.

Courtesy National Archives

Fort Mears afire after the attack.

Courtesy National Archives

Tank farm afire.

Courtesy National Archives

Siems Drake warehouse. Fire fighters are in the
foreground. The SS *Northwestern* is burning on the left.
Courtesy National Archives

Dutch Harbor Naval Air Station June 27, 1942.
The burned out SS *Northwestern* is in the center.
Courtesy National Archives

Damaged Bureau of Indian Affairs hospital.
Courtesy National Archives

CHAPTER V

Interrogation of Commander Masatake Okumiya

After the war, Captain James S. Russell, USN (who retired as an admiral), conducted a series of interrogations in Tokyo of Japanese officers who participated in the Dutch Harbor attack. One of those interrogated was Commander Masatake Okumiya, Imperial Japanese Navy. The interrogation took place October 10, 1945. This is a summary of Commander Okumiya's career and what he told Captain Russell.

Commander Okumiya was an ensign on a light cruiser and destroyer from November 1931 until April 1933 when he enrolled in flight school. Graduating in December 1933, he was promoted to lieutenant (j.g.) and assigned to the Omura Air Group. He served aboard the aircraft carrier *Ryujo* from 1935 through 1937. He participated in air operations in China from 1938 to March 1939. During one engagement, his dive bomber caught fire in a dive and, although he was badly burned about the face and wrists, he made a successful parachute jump. He next served as a lieutenant commander instructor in flying at Kasumigaura. From March 1942 until July 1944, he served as staff officer with the Second, and then the Fourth Air Fleet. From July 1944 until the present, he was assigned to the Naval Air Staff. Commander Okumiya has approximately 2,000 hours flying time.

(All times and dates are Tokyo Zone minus nine.)

On May 30, 1942, the Japanese Second Task Force sortied from Ominato, North Honshu, and set course for a point 20 miles south of Erimo Point on the south coast of Hokkaido. The force was composed of:

2 CVs - *Junyo* and *Ryujo.*
2 CAs - *Takao* and *Maya.*
3 DDs - *Shio, Oboko* and *Akebona.*
1 AO   - *Teiyo Maru,* and later *Toho Maru.*

(CV = aircraft carrier; CA = heavy cruiser; DD = destroyer; AO = oiler)

Departing from Hokkaido, the task force took a Great Circle Route to a position approximately 230 degrees, 400 miles from Dutch Harbor. En route, the task force fueled twice: once on June 1 and again on June 3. Three cruising dispositions were used: one for fair weather, one for poor visibility and one for very poor visibility.

The fair weather disposition consisted of the CVs in a column at a distance of 1,000 meters. *Ryujo* was the guide and at the head of the column. Disposed around the *Ryujo* were the three DDs at 1,500 meters on either beam and ahead. The two CAs were 5,000 meters on either beam of the *Ryujo.* Zig-zagging was used in fair weather.

In poor visibility, the same formation was used except the three DDs formed a column ahead of the *Ryujo* at a distance of 500 meters. The interval from last DD to *Ryujo* was 2,000 meters. In very poor visibility, the two CAs formed astern of the *Junyo* at an interval of 2,000 meters and a distance of 1,000 meters between them. In thick weather, station was kept by position buoys and maneuvering signals were given by VHF radio. No radar was installed at this time.

The mission of the Japanese Second Task Force was to attack ships, planes and shore installations at Dutch Harbor as a diversion to the attack on, and occupation of, Midway, and then to support landing operations in the western Aleutians. (Commander Okumiya said the occupation of Kiska and Attu was planned. However, in a later interview, Captain Sukemitsu Ito, Fifth Fleet Staff Air Officer (see Appendix E), who was responsible for the planning of the occupation, said the occupation of Adak, Kiska and Attu were considered, with the selection to depend on photo reconnaissance. After the Japanese reversal at Midway, Admiral Yamamoto was greatly opposed to the occupation of any of the Aleutians, but was persuaded by Vice Admiral Boshiro Hosogaya, Commander Fifth Fleet, to carry out the occupation of Attu and Kiska.)

The attack on Dutch Harbor was scheduled for June 4, one day earlier than the carrier air attack on Midway.

The task force's speed of advance was limited to 10 to 11 knots due to the slow speed of the accompanying AO. On May 30, 31 and June 1, the force steamed into dense fog. The existence of a mild front was known and the ships attempted to stay ahead of it in the thick weather.

On the morning and afternoon of June 2, and on the morning of June 3, two plane sections scouted ahead to a distance of 130 miles. On the afternoon of June 3, four two-plane sections scouted an area 30 degrees on either side of the task force track to a distance of 250 miles.

The task force had various intelligence reports on American forces from submarine reconnaissance. From a position off the Washington State coast, a submarine had launched a reconnaissance seaplane which scouted Seattle harbor and reported no heavy men-of-war—particularly CVs—there. About May 30, a similar plane, launched from a submarine about 100 miles north of Dutch Harbor, scouted that port and reported only a few small merchant ships present. This plane was damaged due to swells and could not make a scheduled reconnaissance on June 3. Instead, Dutch Harbor was examined by periscope with a negative report made on that date. Two other submarines were patrolling on a line south of Cold Bay. They made no sightings.

A periscope reconnaissance of Kodiak Island was made about the end of May with a negative report. A submarine plane scouted Kiska about May 25 and reported no ships present. The submarine-borne planes maintained radio silence during their flights, with orders to break radio silence only if they were chased by American planes. All reports were made by the mother submarine. The submarine off Seattle, and the one off Kodiak, maintained station for some time. The only contact reported by the Kodiak submarine was that of sighting one large merchant ship on a date which Commander Okumiya did not remember.

During fueling on June 3, crews of the Second Task Force heard the engines of an American plane and thought they saw a flying boat. One of two VFs [fighters], airborne on combat air patrol, gave chase, but lost contact in the poor visibility.

The following air operations were planned for the attack against Dutch Harbor on June 4: The first wave was to be launched at earliest light of dawn (2330, June 3) and the second wave one-half hour later:

1st wave	VF *Ryujo* - 6	*Junyo* - 9	Total = 15
	VB	*Junyo* - 12	Total = 12
	VT *Ryujo* - 9		Total = 9
2nd wave	VF *Ryujo* - 3	*Junyo* - 6	Total = 9

VB *Ryujo* - 6   Total = 6
VT   *Junyo* - 6   Total = 6
Attack seaplanes *Takao* - 2, *Maya* - 2   Total = 4
(VF = fighter; VT = torpedo plane; VB = dive bomber)

The two three-seat seaplanes, one each from *Takao* and *Maya*, were to scout to the eastward.

Weather—fog and low clouds—interfered considerably with the execution of the operation. The first wave was launched on time at a point about 210 degrees, 180 miles from Dutch Harbor. The visibility was from 2,000 to 5,000 meters. One VT from the *Ryujo* had a forced landing in the sea immediately after takeoff. The plane's crew was rescued. As the planes of the first wave flew toward Dutch Harbor, they ran into increasing difficulties due to weather. All of the *Junyo*'s planes turned back, and, of the *Ryujo*'s planes, only three VFs and six VTs got through to the target. The three VFs found no U.S. fighters, so they strafed a Catalina flying boat on the water. The six VTs attacked the radio station, warehouses, pier and shore installations. Of the planes which turned back, two of the three *Ryujo* VFs found a Catalina close to the shore and shot it down. A photo proved this American plane crashed and burned.

One of the nine *Junyo* VFs, after being airborne for about an hour, found a Catalina and, after a chase, shot it down in the vicinity of the carriers. The plane was reported burned. Another of the first wave of VFs found a third Catalina, but it got away in the clouds. One VT from the *Ryujo* found five to six U.S. DDs in Makushin Bay. Upon receipt of this information, the second wave, which had been held on deck due to weather, was launched at about 0900 June 4. All the planes of the second wave turned back except the four seaplanes from the cruisers. Two of those were intercepted over the U.S. DDs, where one was shot down and the other damaged. One of the *Ryujo*'s VFs failed to return after announcing that it was making a forced landing on Akutan. [This was the Zero that was recovered by the U.S.]

(Any Japanese submarine lying north of Dutch Harbor was to pick up downed pilots. In the event of a forced landing, pilots were instructed to attempt landings on one of the small islands off Unalaska Island.)

The final casualty of the day occurred when a three-seat seaplane, returning to its cruiser from a scouting mission to the east, cracked up on landing. The crew was rescued. Of the second wave of carrier planes, all of which turned back due to weather, only three saw any action. These strafed a U.S. submarine off the south coast of Unalaska Island. After the first two VFs made strafing passes, the pilot of the third reported the submarine submerged so that an attack could not be made. During the day, the task force moved toward shore, so that when the second wave landed, their parent carriers were only 100 miles from Dutch Harbor. A combat air patrol of two VFs was maintained over the force through the day. Two-hour patrols were launched alternately by *Ryujo* and *Junyo*. All planes were aboard by approximately 1500 June 4 at which time the task force began a withdrawal by reversing their approach track.

Visibility continued to be poor and weather forecasts indicated weather at Dutch Harbor would probably be worse on the following day. After refueling DDs from the carriers in partial darkness beginning about 0000 June 5, a course was laid to the westward with the idea of making an air reconnaissance of Adak and Atka. At sunrise, Adak bore 300 degrees distance, 250 miles. However the wind velocity was 25 to 30 knots and the sea high, hence no planes were launched. The ships continued westward hoping the weather would improve, but they returned to their sunrise position at about 0300 or 0400. At this time Tokyo reported the weather might be improving at Dutch Harbor. The ships headed there. One or two PBYs were sighted fairly early in the morning, and one about two hours later. At 0900, two VTs were launched from *Ryujo* for a weather reconnaissance of Dutch Harbor. These planes found one U.S. DD south of Unalaska Island. They reported weather in the vicinity of Dutch Harbor was not good, but a little better than the preceding day. It was decided to launch a second attack against Dutch Harbor.

Meanwhile, various air attacks were carried out against the task force. Visibility was poor and the recognition of enemy planes as to type was uncertain. Commander Okumiya thought only PBYs and B-17s were involved. Four protective fighters were launched. They chased and shot down one PBY and believed they damaged a second. Various planes were fired upon by the ships of the task force. The *Takao*, well out to the left flank of the formation, shot down a B-17, taking one prisoner. Two bombs missed one DD by about 500 meters. One bomb hit well clear of the *Junyo*. Some planes, which Commander Okumiya thought were B-17s, but which could have been B-26s, dropped torpedoes in the water about 200 meters on her port quarter. They did not detonate.

Between these attacks and about 1100, the second day's attack against Dutch Harbor was launched. Because of poor weather only the most skilled pilots were allowed to participate. Only one wave was launched:

VF *Ryujo* - 6	*Junyo*	-	9	Total =	15
VB	*Junyo*	-	11	Total =	11
VT	*Ryujo*	-	6	Total =	6

All planes reached the target, but reported en route they dodged considerable cloud masses. No U.S. fighters were encountered at the target; Japanese VFs strafed ground targets. The VBs and VTs bombed the aircraft hangar, oil tanks, one transport that was docked, and warehouses. Photographs showed a large fire which they believed to be the burning hangar.

The west end of Unalaska Island was the rallying and rendezvous point for the attack group from the *Junyo*. When they arrived at this rendezvous point they were attacked by about 10 U.S. fighters. In the ensuing dog fights, two VFs and two VBs from the *Junyo* were shot down. It was estimated that five or six U.S. fighters were shot down. The *Junyo* planes reported a large U.S. field on the east end of Umnak Island, the location of which was hitherto unknown to the Japanese.

The *Ryujo* recovered all of her planes about an hour before sunset. Due to the delay involved in the dog fight over Umnak Pass, the *Junyo*'s planes were late returning and did not land until sunset. Her losses were the two VFs and two VBs shot down over Umnak Pass. Another VB's radio receiver was knocked out and the plane became separated from the others during the fight. Its transmitter was working. It called in several times reporting fuel remaining and requesting navigational assistance which *Junyo* could not give because the plane could not receive. It was presumed this plane went down at sea. Total losses for the second day's attack were two VFs and three VBs, all from *Junyo*. No surface ship of the Second Task Force was damaged during either day of the Dutch Harbor attacks.

Tokyo provided weather forecasting for the Dutch Harbor attack. It was excellent as far as wind and general conditions were concerned, but the forecasting of fog was poor. The weather front used by the task force did not exist at first. Later a low pressure area developed, helping conceal the force but making scouting difficult.

Intelligence: Second Task Force estimated 30 large land planes at Kodiak, some large planes at Nome; no land planes, but about 12 patrol bomber seaplanes at Dutch Harbor.

The task force thought a small field existed at Dutch Harbor, but had no knowledge of fields on Umnak or on the Alaskan Peninsula. It was believed, without specific intelligence, that seaplanes could base at Atka and Adak, and at both these places, terrain could be found upon which an airfield could be built.

After the second Dutch Harbor attack on June 5 (June 4, Alaska date), the task force retired to a point about 600 miles south of Kiska where the *Zuiho*, together with two battle cruisers (sister ships which Commander Okumiya thought may have been the *Kongo* and *Haruna*) and four DDs joined. The *Zuiho* had been with a detached group of ships at the battle of Midway and had survived that action. This augmented task force cruised between June 7 and 17 south of Kiska with the object of cutting off any U.S. carrier force which might be sent from Midway to interfere with the Japanese landing operations on Kiska and Attu.

No vessel from the Second Task Force went in to Kiska, nor was air cover provided over Kiska by carrier planes. However an interception of U.S. planes that might attack Kiska was planned, and the task force force moved to a point 250 miles south of the island for that purpose. Weather, however, prevented the launching of any fighters for the planned interception. When weather permitted, two training flights were launched daily—four planes in the morning and four planes in the afternoon. Air searches were also made when practicable. One of the latter extended into the Bering Sea to a distance of 100 miles north of Kiska about the time the interception was being planned.

The Second Task Force exchanged recognition signals with the seaplane carrier *Kimikawa* when she was en route to Kiska. When that ship arrived in Kiska on June 15 and had discharged her seaplane fighters, reconnaissance planes, their fuel and other logistic materials, the task force returned to Ominato where it arrived on about June 23.

The task force sortied again on or about June 30, reinforced by the addition of the aircraft carrier *Zuikaku*, a survivor of the Coral Sea action in which the *Shoho* was lost. (CVs with Second Task Force were: *Ryujo, Junyo, Zuiho* and *Zuikaku*.)

Anchorage Daily Times

FOR VICTORY
Buy U.S. Bonds Stamps

SERVE IN SILENCE
Do Not Reveal
Military Information

"READ BY ALASKANS EVERYWHERE"

TWENTY-SIXTH YEAR   ANCHORAGE, ALASKA, THURSDAY, JUNE 1, 1942   PRICE TEN CENTS

CONTINUE 11-2 O'CLOCK BLACKOUTS; SILENCE MARKS DUTCH HARBOR RAID

R.A.F. Stages 94th Raid On Bremen

Deadly Night Flying Armada's Continue Blasting Program

LONDON, June 4, (AP)—British bombers heavily blasted firemen, Germany's second seaport, while the British commandos fruitfully scouted the Boulogne and Letouquet area of Hitler's French coastal, defense over night.

Government agencies announced that the Bremen raid, the 94th on that city during the war, was linked with an attack on the Dieppe docks.

The air ministry announced that 10 bombers and two fighters were missing after the night's operations. Strong RAF forces flew through moonlit skies to strike targets at Bremen such as shipbuilding and submarine yards and docks, railways, steel works, oil refining installations and aircraft factories.

It was a follow-up of the mass raids on Cologne and Essen.

Only Hamburg ranks ahead of Bremen as a German maritime center.

Meanwhile, blackfaced commandos reported by navy warships and protected on the withdrawal by RAF fighters, stabbed across the Dover strait after midnight on a reconnaissance raid.

The daring commandos were declared to have produced "valuable information." Casualties during their operations were declared slight.

Five Arrested For Failure To Leave Streets

Arrested during the blackout period Wednesday night five men were heard by City Magistrate Karl Drager this morning, and fined a total of $80.

The men, according to police, were charged with being drunk and refusing to leave the streets during the blackout. Ralph Konway was fined $25, Carl Carlson $5, Iran Selver $15, John Vzan, $10, and Allen Brown, $25.

Heydrich Dies, Fear Hundreds Will Be Shot

BERLIN, June 4 (AP)—Reinhard Heydrich, 38, Reichsprotector in Bohemia and Moravia, died at Prague this morning of wounds suffered in an attempt upon his life May 27.

It was announced officially that the assassination of the man, who was known among scores of millions of Europe's oppressed peoples as "Der Henker," the hangman, was expected to bring swift reprisals in addition to the 162 who have already been slain.

Swift reprisals were expected in Czech circles.

Czechs Used Automatic Army Rifles In Shooting

LONDON, June 4 (AP)—It was asserted by a Czech source in London today that automatic rifles were used by two men to shoot Heydrich. The guns were taken from the ordnance of the disbanded Czech army. The men possibly dropped by parachute to shoot the German official.

British Route Axis Force

By Associated Press

British imperial armored forces were reported today to have routed axis soldiers from their desert stronghold in a fierce engagement while Free French Allies held to the last against efforts of General Rommel to seize the key position of Bir Hacheim.

The middle east command's communique said British forces attacking last night (June 2) drove the enemy out of Tamar, 21 miles southwest of Tobruk and six miles west of Knightsbridge, center around which occurred the most fighting in this latest Libyan campaign.

General Rommel apparently desires to capture Bir Hacheim, at the southern-end of his severed line that cuts sideline of Knightsbridge, and impossible for the British to counter-attack that tiny oasis about 50 miles southwest of Tobruk.

COUNCIL TO MEET
Anchorage city council will meet tonight at 8 o'clock, according to Mayor William A. Stolt. The session called for last night was cancelled.

MAKE WAY FOR BUTCH, HE MUST HAVE A DAILY DUNK

... apparently separated from ... mother's life took the spot ... of grease with him abo ... treated much ...

At the White House, President Roosevelt pins a Congressional Medal of Honor on Brig. Gen. James H. (Jimmy) Doolittle, at the same time revealing it was he who led a squadron of volunteer flyers on a "highly successful" bombing raid on Tokyo and the mainland of Japan. From left, Lt. Gen. H. H. Arnold, Chief of the Army Air Force; President Roosevelt, Mrs. Doolittle; Gen. George Marshall, Chief of Staff.

FAST AND DEADLY

Somewhere on the Pacific Coast these deathdealing P-38 fighters are rounding an aviation tower in never ceasing maneuvers that keep their pilots in fine fettle for action against a venturesome enemy. Built by Lockheed, they are the Army's most high-powered, most heavily armed combat plane. Their Liquid cooled motors, supercharged for high altitude work, give them 2,700 horsepower and a top speed of 404 miles an hour. Cannon and machine guns are grouped in the nose, firing in a straight line instead of converging in a cone as with wing-mounted guns.

Allied Subs Sink Loaded Troop Ship

ALLIED HEADQUARTERS, AUSTRALIA, June 4 (AP)—Allied submarines sank an armed transport of 8,000 tons with the probable loss of all troops and two heavily loaded supply ships in the Indian and damaged enemy waters, a communique issued here last night said.

Ships sunk totalled 22,000 tons. It was estimated that the Japs might have lost 12,000 troops on the transport.

The communique did not specify the time covered by the operations but said the sinkings occurred during a raid on enemy shipping lines.

The Allied headquarters also announced that Jap submarines had sunk one ship off the coast of Australia.

Prime Minister Curtin said three of four Japanese submarines that entered the Sydney harbor last Sunday were sunk before they could make an attack. An any shipping. Curtin told Parliament that the fourth submarine alone was able to fire its torpedoes but that it was also sunk before she got away. It had been previously reported that only three of the midget submarines were sunk.

Pays $50 Fine For Recklessness

Lloyd Mattingley, arrested early Wednesday morning by city police and charged with reckless driving, speeding, failure to stop at stop signs, and careening from an alley on to private property, paid a $50 fine in magistrate's court this morning.

Alaskan Wild Life Man Dies

WASHINGTON, D.C., June 4, (AP)—Glen Clinton Leach, 70, who for 24 years was chief of the fish culture division of the Fish and Wildlife Service, died Wednesday after a long illness. He served at stations in Afognak and Yes Bay, both in Alaska.

Freeze Sale Of All Bikes

Anchorage rationing board is notifying local bicycle dealers of the freezing of new or used adult bicycles for purposes of sale or rental, on authority of OPA.

A new adult bicycle is described as any pedal-propelled, non-motor, two-wheeled vehicle with a frame, measurement of more than 17 inches from the center of the crank to the top of the seat post mast, which has feet...

Warns of Steel Shortage Soon

WASHINGTON, D.C. June 4 (AP)—A previously planned 16,000,000-ton steel expansion program will be cut 30 to 35 per cent, a top war official announced today, because of material shortage.

American industry must prepare to "patch and pray" to keep their existing equipment at work. The statements were made by William Batt—at his press conference who gave a frank and un-encouraging review of the country's looming shortages.

Governor Lauds Alaska Defense

Official silence in both Washington and Tokyo continued today to cover the details of yesterday's two air raids on Dutch Harbor, but Anchorage citizens were warned to remain on the alert.

The Dutch Harbor situation was covered by brief naval communiques, but by no word from army forces involved.

The navy communique, issued at Washington, summarized the results of the raid as follows:

Japanese planes raided the Navy base at least twice yesterday, once at about 6 a.m., the second time at noon.

The first attack was made by four bombers and 15 fighter planes. No estimate of the number of planes in the second attack was given.

Damage to the base was not detailed by the Navy as a few warehouses set afire. Casualties were also described as few.

The navy said its communiques were based on reports received up to 6 p.m. yesterday and did not cover possible hostilities during the night.

No estimates of what, if any, damage our fighting forces received or gave out were made.

The Tokyo radio was completely silent about the raid although it continued its usual budget of propaganda about other fronts.

In Juneau, Governor Ernest Gruening expressed satisfaction with the activities of the army and navy during the first attack on the territory.

His statement follows:

"To the people of Alaska:

"The anticipated air raid on Alaska began this morning with an attack by Jap planes on Dutch Harbor.

"Our Army and Navy are rendering an excellent account of themselves. All civilian defense units should remain on the alert.

"Details as deemed advisable will be released in time by military authorities."

For Anchorage, the way tonight, will mean an other total blackout," Sidney C. Raynor, director of civilian defense, ordered the blackout on instructions from local military commanders.

Householders, merchants, motorists and pedestrians affected the most complete blackout Anchorage has yet seen when last night at 11 o'clock the city went into total darkness, city and Civilian Defense officials declared today.

Immediately after 11 o'clock Wednesday patrolling officers, volunteers, block and district wardens reminded many residents to darken "their homes. Downtown merchants cooperated fully.

"All persons responsible for light of any kind showing during the blackout hours of 11 p.m. to 2 a.m., will be warned once and on second violation will be hailed into court, authorities said.

While the blackout in the city met with favor, the area just beyond the city limits and near the city dump did not fare so well.

Two tire alarms were turned in, the first at 11:10 p.m., the second at 1:10 a.m. On the first call firemen found a shack blazing and several small fires burning on the city dump. On the early morning call they found a second shack afire.

Three men, Otto and Sammy Erickson and Bert Orien were found in a nearby shack and were arrested and charged with being drunk.

The Erickson men were sentenced to five days in jail by City Magistrate Karl Drager this morning. Orien was fined $25.

In announcing total blackout each night until further notice the following warnings are again given:

Automobiles must keep headlights dark.

Street lights and outdoor signs must be dark.

Homes must be darkened.

No light coverings will be permitted.

Smoking on the streets is permitted.

Penalize West Alaska Shipping

SEATTLE, June 4 (AP)—Pacific Northwest defense authorities said today the Alaska Steamship line had placed an embargo on all civilian-directed and passenger traffic west of Kodiak. The restriction, affecting Alaska ports west of Kodiak, cover a frank and un-encouraging review of the country's looming shortages.

CHAPTER VI

War Diary

(This is the war diary of Captain Leslie E. Gehres, of Patrol Wing Four, covering events from May 27, 1942, through June 30, 1942. The diary was probably prepared by Lieutenant Commander Paul Foley, who was commander of VP Squadron 42. Captain Gehres occasionally used Foley as his advanced staff operations officer [ADSTOP]. The war diary is presented here as it was written. Classified at the time, the writer reports what he knew, and what others told him of the attack. As a result, his subjective analysis reflects the varied perspectives of the participants. He was not attempting to be vague.)

For reasons explained below this "diary" is submitted in narrative form. Hereafter it will be in the form recently prescribed by Commander Patrol Wings, Pacific Fleet.

Events followed upon each other so rapidly during the above period, and Commander Patrol Wing Four was shifted to the Alaska Area with only such personnel and equipment as could be carried in a limited number of aircraft ready for combat service, that it was impossible to keep a regular war diary day-by-day due to the lack of clerical assistance and the fact that every working moment (which for nearly three weeks averaged over twenty hours out of each twenty-four), was devoted entirely to planning, directing and controlling active air operations against the enemy.

This diary therefore is submitted in narrative form, prepared from notes and memos made at the time, the file of official despatches, and my own recollections. It is accompanied by a smooth plot of the first phase of the Aleutian Campaign, with accompanying legend, and a tabulation of all enemy contacts and actions in which any units of Patrol Wing Four were involved. It should be understood that this tabulation and the plot legend were prepared long after the events; many [of] the reports were received days late and even now they are not complete. The operating units have been operating from advance bases, from many wide-spread dispersal points, with only meager improvised communication facilities. Squadron Commanders sometimes do not see pilots for several days. Some are lost before they can be interviewed.

A certain amount of background is introduced in this narrative to indicate how little initial preparation was possible. Regular patrols were carried on in the Northwestern Sector [West Coast of continental U.S.] up to the day preceding the Wing Commander's [Captain Gehres] departure for Alaska.

About 18 May it became evident that there was in prospect increased operations in the Aleutian area which would involve Patrol Wing Four; Naval Intelligence having [been] informed of certain Japanese plans in that direction. The first preliminary move was to request and obtain authority from Commander Northwest Sea Frontier to transfer all aircraft torpedoes and torpedo personnel in the Northwest Sea Frontier to such Alaskan bases as Commander Patrol Wing Four selected. On 21 May 1942, the Commander-in-Chief, U.S. Navy established Task Force Eight and the various command relationships which were to exist between Naval and Army authorities. Arrangements were made to shift four Catalinas from Patrol Squadron 43 at Alameda to Tongue Point to assist in the patrols of the Northwestern Sector in order to place a total of twenty Catalinas in Alaska. These arrangements were at one time cancelled and not until 25 May were they carried out, thus releasing Patrol Squadron 41 [Lieutenant Commander Paul Foley, CO] from routine patrols on 26 May. It was also necessary at this time to rush six Catalinas to Alameda for the installation of radar equipment.

In order to provide for a continuing control of offshore patrols in the Northwestern Sector by the remaining Navy planes and the allocated Army squadrons, it was decided to leave in Seattle the Wing Commander's Staff Operations officer, two communication officers and necessary enlisted personnel, while Commander Patrol Wing Four with the remainder of the Wing Staff and administrative personnel moved to Kodiak. Due to transportation difficulties only those few officers who could fly to Kodiak plus a small advance contingent on the [USS] *Gillis* were available at the commencement of active hostilities. Badly needed radiomen and radio equipment did not arrive until the first phase of the campaign was over.

On 25 May, Commander Patrol Wing Four was advanced to the temporary rank of Captain, U.S.N., the Wing tactical officer Lieutenant McCracken and the Wing communications officer Lieutenant Picken were advanced to the temporary rank[s] of Lieutenant Commander. On 27 May 1942, the Wing Commander, accompanied by the above named officers, proceeded with Patrol Squadron Forty-One to Kodiak, arriving about 1730. The Wing Commander reported immediately to Commander Alaskan Sector and to Brigadier General [William O.] Butler, Air Corps, U.S. Army, Commanding General 11th Air Force, who had been named the Commander of all air forces, Army and Navy, attached to Task Force Eight. On 28 May, Rear Admiral [Robert A.] Theobald, U.S.N., Commander of the North Pacific Force, arrived in Kodiak and in an immediately called conference explained his general plan of organization and operation to all concerned.

Patrol Wing Four was designated as an air search group (Task Group Eight point One of Task Force Eight). Patrol plans to utilize to the maximum the available seaplanes were worked out and approved by Commander Task Force Eight. That evening, Commander Task Force Eight operation order 1-42, and Commander Task Group Eight point One operation order 1-42 were issued. The squadrons and tenders of Patrol Wing Four moved out immediately in accordance with the provisions of these orders, and on 29 May the regular patrols were instituted.

It was immediately apparent that there were not sufficient tenders attached to the Wing and request was made [to] Commander Patrol Wings, Pacific Fleet, to dispatch the USS *Hulbert* from Hawaii to Alaska. This request was acceded to and the *Hulbert* was dispatched immediately. Request was made [to] Commander Northwest Sea Frontier for the immediate release of the remaining planes of Patrol Squadron 41 as it was also apparent that these planes would be urgently needed in Alaska to replace expected operational and combat losses. Extended overnight patrols in the Aleutian area have never before been attempted and many pilots in both squadrons had little, if any, experience in Alaskan and Aleutian operations. Great reliance was, of necessity, placed on the radar installations not only to prevent collisions with fog-shrouded mountains, but to make the actual searches effective, as there were not available sufficient planes, nor enough visibility, to permit close visual search. As later events proved, this reliance was fully justified. Until the enemy ships were located in Kiska, every contact was made by radar, then developed visually.

On 29 May, information was received from the Commander-in-Chief, Pacific Fleet, of the composition of the Japanese Northern Force which was expected to attempt to seize bases in the Aleutian area. Information was later received of the approximate time of departure of this force from Ominato and the opinion given that this force could arrive at Kiska on 31 May or 1 June, but that in view of forces believed to be en route to attack Midway it was assumed that Unalaska was the objective of the enemy northern force and that air attack on Dutch Harbor should be expected between 31 May and 3 June, and a landing attack between 1 and 4 June.

On 29 May, the first positive sight contact of an enemy submarine was made by aircraft out of Dutch Harbor. On 29 May, a Catalina investigated Atka which had not been heard from by radio for two days and found everything to be normal there. The same plane landed at Kanaga and provisioned the Navy unit there.

The communications facilities and personnel at the Naval Air Station, Kodiak, were found to be entirely inadequate to carry the load imposed by the presence on the station of the operating headquarters of Patrol Wing Four and the 11th Air Force. With the full authority and the cooperation of the Commanding Officer of the Station, the Staff communication officer of Patrol Wing Four took over the communication department and, with the assistance of a few Wing radiomen and some equipment, which had, by this time, arrived at Kodiak, reorganized and took charge of communications. There was an acute shortage of trained radiomen, receivers, transmitters and coding machines, but during the crowded days which followed, the Patrol Wing Four's communications did function and were in fact the only sure and rapid means of communications between the various and wide-spread units of both the Naval and Army Air Forces.

From 29 May to, and including, 2 June, the Patrol Squadrons and units at advance bases operated with increasing efficiency as the bases became organized and equipment began to be received and the pilots gained experience and confidence in flying night radar patrols. There were increasing R.D.F. [Radio Direction Finder] indications of the presence of numerous Japanese submarines in the Aleutian area. On 2 June, information was received that there were radio indications of enemy carrier aircraft operating on a line due south of Kiska, and not over 400 miles distance therefrom.

A study of the situation based on this radio information, the composition of the attacking force as reported by Commander-in-Chief, United States Navy, and Commander-in-Chief, United States Pacific Fleet, their assumed objective and the approximate time of departure from Ominato, led to the following assumptions: That the composition of the force involved, the individual and formation speeds of the various types, the nature of their mission, the physical nature of their objective, and the methods previously employed by the enemy, indicated a logical division of the forces as follows:

(a) "Southern Covering Force" 3 CA [heavy cruisers] 1 *Ryujo* CV [aircraft carrier] and 4 *Hibiki* DD [destroyers] as screen and plane guards. This would provide a fast homogeneous air striking force to approach south of the Aleutian chain. If the Aleutian attack was intended as a diversion, the enemy would provide for the success of the ruse and expect to find some U.S. Fleet forces operating in the Aleutian area and probably south of the Islands. The Southern Covering Force's mission would therefore be first, to cover the approach of the remainder of the force in the Bering Sea, and secondly, coordinate an attack on the Aleutian bases with an attack from the north.

(b) A Convoy Covering Force consisting of two CA, two XCA's and six *Shiguri* DD to approach from the West along the northern side of the Aleutian chain to cover the transports and train which would be farther north in the Bering Sea.

(c) The remainder of the force consisting of transports, tankers, landing boat carriers, escorted by two CL [light cruisers] was believed to be headed for the Bering Sea where it could take up a position to descend upon the Bering Sea side of the islands selected for landing attacks when the Southern and Convoy Covering Forces had prepared the way.

The southern coasts of the Aleutian Islands offer practically no possibilities of landing while the northern coasts offer many fine beaches. It was unreasonable to believe that a large and comparatively slow train would be brought in south of the Islands and then attempt the few narrow passes to launch landing attacks upon the northern beaches. It was further assumed that the presence of the destroyers in the force would require refueling at sea somewhere between the Commondorski [Komandorski] Islands [of the USSR] and Attu. Assuming that the slowest force would not advance faster than 13 knots, that the fueling would take at least one day, and that the advance would generally be by the most direct route, that is either a great circle course for the Southern Force to a point south of Unalaska, or by a great circle course to a refueling point east of the end of the Aleutian chain, plus the line of position and distance limit given by Intelligence of carrier-based aircraft operating south of Kiska, plus a study of the weather map which indicated an approaching front with a fifty-mile belt of rain and mist in advance, plus increasing R.D.F. indications of extensive submarine activity north of the Aleutians led to the belief that at least a part, probably the so-called Covering Force, would be between midnight on 2 June and noon on 3 June in the area bounded by latitudes forty-five and fifty north and longitude one hundred seventy-six to one hundred and eighty degrees west. From a consideration of the foregoing it was believed that an attack could, and probably would, be made on Dutch Harbor on the morning of 3 June, and certainly not later than the morning of 4 June. This reasoning, and the conclusions drawn therefrom, demonstrated by chart diagrams and the weather map, were presented orally to Commander Alaskan Sector and the Commanding General, 11th Air Force, about 1500 on 2 June.

At 030217 Zed [June 3], a radio message was sent to Umnak to be delivered to the radar-equipped Army B-17, which was believed to be there, as follows: "Search area bounded latitude forty-five to fifty longitude one seventy-six west to one hundred eighty earliest daylight time 3 June." Due to the difficulties of communication with Umnak, and a confusion there as to the detail and employment of certain Army aircraft, the pilot and plane, for whom the message was intended, failed to receive it. Certain later assumptions as to position made from an unidentified contact report were, to some extent, faulty due to a lack of knowledge that this message had not been received in time and the search was not initiated until 0730W instead of 0230W. The pilot for whom the message was intended was dispatched on a different mission and a relief plane landing on the field received the message late, but the pilot accepted the orders and took off on the mission. Some five days later it was discovered, by a process of elimination, what had happened to the message and who the pilot was. This will be noted later in this diary.

On the morning of 3 June, Dutch Harbor was attacked by enemy aircraft. The first warning of the impending attack was flashed by the USS *Gillis,* whose radar equipment, entire battery and fire control system were manned on a twenty-four hour basis. Twenty minutes before [the] first plane appeared, the *Gillis* radar operator picked up an approaching formation of aircraft twenty-four and one-half miles away, and when the first airplane appeared over the hills back of Unalaska, the *Gillis* opened fire with every gun, bringing down one high bomber and one fighter of this wave, and by a well-directed fire at a Zero fighter which had strafed and was attempting to finish off a PBY taxiing on the water, drove off the fighter and undoubtedly saved the remainder of the crew of the PBY. During the attack on Dutch Harbor and immediately after it, there were numerous contacts between Catalinas and enemy aircraft. The Catalinas were mostly returning from overnight patrols, but due to the system of making thirty minute E.T.A. reports with an affirmative or negative reply, it proved possible to bring in the planes, refuel them and get them out

again without exposing them to the enemy fighters at the base. One
Catalina encountered two enemy single engine observation planes,
shot down one and apologized for letting the other escape.

At about ten thirty in the morning, Kodiak time, contact report
was received from an Army plane under the call of 0V28 which
decoded as follows: "Affirmative carrier large bombing plane on deck."
No speed, course or position was given. Despite every effort to reach
the plane by radio, no amplifying report was ever received. It was
assumed that the plane making the contact report was the B-17 to
whom had been given the special mission of searching the area
previously described, as the call 0V28 was the one assigned to the
plane on the Aleutian Island Patrol. As was discovered several days
later, two Army planes were on this day using the same call. The
plane which was later determined to have made the contact report,
piloted by Captain [Thomas F.] Mansfield, who was later lost before
personal interview could be had, was the one who received the orders intended for Captain [Russell] Cone [commander of an Army
Air Force B-17 squadron], and took off at 0730W to search the area
indicated. He had made the Aleutian patrol the day before, using
the radio call 0V28, and did not know when he took off that Captain
Cone had been sent north of the Aleutians to run down a strong
radio carrier aircraft bearing, or that Captain Cone was also using
the call 0V28. The contact was first thought to be much farther
west due to the belief that the plane having made it had taken off
early as directed. Actually this plane did not take off until 0730W
and thus the contact was made much closer in as indicated on the
plot which accompanies this diary. As soon as the attack on Dutch
Harbor developed, every effort was made to get the PBYs in, refuel
them and get them out to search. No contacts with enemy surface
vessels were made until at about 1700 Kodiak time when a garbled
message was received from a PBY two forty-five north longitude,
one hundred sixty-four west. No amplifying report was received.
Three days later the reason for this failure was explained when the
rescued pilot was returned to Kodiak and reported. He had made a
contact by radar with four large enemy ships. [These were most
likely CVs *Ryujo* and *Junyo*, and CAs *Maya* and *Takao*. Also part of
this group might have included DDs *Ushio*, *Oboro* and *Akebono*.] As
he came within about twenty-five miles of the concentration, an
indication of an approaching plane was seen on the radar screen
and followed rapidly down until it disappeared as at an indicated
four miles. Immediately thereafter he was heavily attacked from the
starboard rear, and the plane literally riddled with .30 caliber ar-
mored-piercing bullets followed by a single cannon-shot hit which
took out half his forward starboard strut. The .30 caliber fire badly

wounded one man, damaged his radio, shot away his rudder control, damaged one aileron, punctured his gasoline tank, and started a fire in the tunnel compartment. At the time of this contact, he was flying in the lower part of the overcast in a heavy snow storm. The attacking plane came abeam of the starboard blister and the gunner got off a short burst at it. As it disappeared in the snow storm, Lieutenant (j.g.) [L. D.] Campbell [VP-42], the pilot, pulled up and turned away. After about forty-five minutes, the fire in the tunnel compartment was extinguished, the wounded man bandaged and made comfortable. It was seen that no fire was resulting from the leaking gasoline tank and that the plane could be handled sufficiently well without the rudder to continue. This pilot made four more radar contacts with the enemy force which he described as showing in the radar screen as four ships [two CVs: *Ryujo and Junyo*; two CAs: *Takao* and *Maya*] in a diamond formation. Each time as he came to between twenty-five and twenty miles of the contact, there was an indication of a plane approaching him. He found that by making a sharp ninety degree turn the plane disappeared and he was not attacked. After making four such contacts, his plane captain told him he had only about one-half hours fuel left, whereupon he pulled up through the overcast and laid a course for Scotch Cap. Fifteen miles south of Scotch Cap [Akutan Harbor?], his gasoline became exhausted and he made a forced dead-stick landing on the water. After stopping the holes in the plane with cotton and rags, and getting the auxiliary power unit functioning—the bilge pump going, and with all hands except the wounded—sufficiently for the radioman to retransmit the initial contact report and the fact that the plane was down on the water badly damaged. Before the position of the plane could be given, the radio gave out again. This report was garbled and the transmission was poor, and for several days it was believed that the plane was down in the vicinity of the original contact, and a plane which was a few hours later reported as sighted down in the actual position of Campbell's plane was believed to be an entirely different plane. This confusion was not cleared up until 6 June when Lieutenant (j.g.) Campbell was returned to Kodiak by the small boat which rescued him. During the period between landing and rescuing, Lieutenant (j.g.) Campbell rigged his plane for towing, he having been dropped a note by a squadron-mate, that a boat was on its way to him. When the towing was attempted by the rescue boat the plane filled with water. They therefore abandoned it, and after setting it afire with machine gun tracer fire, sunk it.

It later appeared that, from some source to the writer unknown, Fort Glenn had received a contact report indicating an enemy in the same position where Lieutenant (j.g.) Campbell had made contact.

This report eventually reached Commander Patrol Wing Four, but only after the lapse of about six hours and, as at the time of its receipt, Lieutenant (j.g.) Campbell's story was not yet known, it was not seen as confirming his radar contact. However (and this was not known until the following day), a formation of B-26s took off from Otter Point Field toward this position, but failed to find anything in the fog and snow. This is easily understandable as Lieutenant (j.g.) Campbell's series of contacts give a line of positions on the chart which indicate that the enemy formation was proceeding east by north, south of Unalaska at a speed of 18 knots, and the position toward which Captain [Robert] Meals went with the B-26s was two and one-half hours behind [the] formation.

On the evening of 3 June, I [probably Lieutenant Commander Foley] transmitted a message to Commander Task Force Eight in which I stated that my estimate as of 1730W that date, was that the attack on Dutch Harbor had come from at least two small carriers probably in the Bering Sea (actually they were south of Unalaska, but had not been definitely contacted) [and] believe large carrier south of Aleutians in the outer limits of sector 10 heading east to attack Dutch from the south on early 4 June.

At 041650 on 4 June 1942, a PBY piloted by Lieutenant (j.g.) [Marshall C.] Freerks [VP-42] reported: "three radar contact, one sight contact, course 96 position 171-145007." This was followed at 041725 with a report: "Course 0150 two carrier guards, one behind, one starboard." At 0141750, the same plane reported as follows: "As previously reported, enemy carrier, two destroyers, course 150, true speed not known." This plane also sent a complete weather description giving the ceiling, visibility, course, direction of the wind and state of sea. Having been on patrol all night, and being short on fuel, this Catalina was ordered to return to Umnak, and a relief plane started out. Before leaving, the pilot attempted to bomb the carrier, but was driven off by anti-aircraft fire with his plane damaged and one engine out of commission. Contact was lost about 041755.

At the time contact was made, two PBYs loaded the night before with one torpedo each for ferrying to Umnak Field, and dispersed for the night to Akutan, were in the air circling Umnak Pass awaiting clearance to take the torpedoes to Umnak. The senior pilot, Lieutenant Commander [Charles E. "Cy"] Perkins [VP-42], hearing Lieutenant (j.g.) Freerks' contact report, radioed him: "Make MOs on 440 Kcs, high strength," and immediately started with the other torpedo plane [PBY armed with a torpedo] for the position of the enemy. Upon learning that contact had been lost, Lieutenant Commander Perkins placed himself and accompanying plane on a scouting line to regain contact. At 042100, Lieutenant Commander Perkins regained contact with the enemy and sent the following contact report: "Contact 13V3 CA 2 DD, course 360, speed 15, bearing 215, distance 165 Dutch Harbor. Enemy in cruising disposition, carriers surrounded, few planes on deck, visibility fair. This is the same force previously reported, take bearings on me." At 042125, he reported enemy changed course to 200 degrees, speed 20 knots. At 04220, he reported position 135 miles, bearing 208, from the field at 2200 Zed, course 060, speed 15. At 042318, Lieutenant Commander Perkins, having been ordered back because of a shortage of fuel, and a relief plane being on the way, he attempted to torpedo the carrier. He was heavily struck by anti-aircraft fire and one engine put out of commission. He hurriedly fired his torpedo at the heavy cruiser whose fire had damaged his plane. [As a result of] the plane, being nearly out of control, the torpedo attack was not successful.

It is to be noted here that Lieutenant Commander Perkins stayed in contact with this enemy for more than two hours, making repeated position and contact reports and making radio "MOs" between reports.

The enemy carrier and cruisers then apparently maneuvered within a circle about 30 miles in diameter from 042200 to 050150 (a period of three hours and fifty minutes). A relief attacking PBY made repeated reports of their movements during this time, and finally attempted to bomb the carrier's deck, but was struck by anti-aircraft fire and oil and fuel lines cut in one engine. It was during this time that one army pilot of a B-26 came suddenly upon the carrier formation and apparently not realizing the opportunity he had for a "browning" torpedo shot, attempted to circle the formation to get a clear shot at the carrier. Being driven off by anti-aircraft, he climbed and eventually dive-bombed the carrier with a torpedo which, naturally, did not explode. He reported the position of the enemy as bearing 210, distance 120 miles from Otter Point Field, course 330, speed 25, and composition as one CV large [*Ryuno*], one CV small [*Junyo*], two CA [*Takao* and *Maya*] and three DDs. It is my opinion that he mistook one heavy cruiser for a carrier, as all the Naval aviators in contact with this formation throughout the day had consistently reported one carrier and three heavy cruisers.

At about 050515, two B-26s from Captain Meals' flight made contact with the formation. Each fired one torpedo at the CA. Captain Meals' torpedo was reported as having been seen to hit and detonate against the bow. The other torpedo was last seen running in the direction of the ship. The enemy's course at this time was 360, speed 25 knots. Contact was then lost.

At 050355, Dutch Harbor was again attacked by Japanese planes which undoubtedly came from the carriers still maneuvering in this small area south of Umnak. At 050717, contact with the carrier group was again regained by Captain [John L.] Marks, AC, U.S. Army, in a B-17 which had been attached to the Navy search group. He, in company with a B-17 which he believed to have been piloted by Captain Mansfield (he reports that the accompanying plane was apparently unable to communicate by radio) first sighted enemy aircraft flying south through Umnak Pass, lined out their course, followed them and came upon the carrier group (position indicated in the attached plot). Captain Mansfield dove directly down and was never seen again. It is presumed that he was shot down. Captain Marks pulled up into the overcast after getting a good line of the formation, made a run above the overcast, and dropped four 500 pound bombs in train. Captain Marks, his navigator and his crew agree that the blast indications of the exploding bombs indicated three drops in the water, and one hit on something. This was the last contact with this enemy force.

It was about this time that the USS *Williamson,* proceeding through Umnak Pass, was attacked by a formation of five or six Zero fighters. Two fighters cruised parallel to the *Williamson's* course which held her fire until they turned in on her. Her fire then was so heavy and so accurately directed that both planes turned away without hitting the *Williamson.* Both were seen to be hit and were streaming gas and smoke. Actual destruction was not claimed, although two planes were seen to crash in the water. There was a dog-fight going on overhead at this moment between other Zeros and pursuit from Otter Point, and it was possible that they were from the fight going on overhead. Another Zero dove out of the clouds directly overhead and on the *Williamson* while her fire was directed at the first two attacking planes. This plane succeeded in delivering an effective fire on the bridge and forecastle gun of the *Williamson.* Twelve minor casualties resulted with a number of .50 caliber armor piercing holes through the *Williamson's* bridge structure, forecastle deck and side. The Commanding Officer, Lieutenant Commander Kivette, removing his heavy sheep's wool lined great coat several hours later, found three spent 50 caliber armor piercing projectiles in the sheepskin lining. He had maneuvered and fought his ship and directed its fire from an exposed position on his "tin can" bridge.

It was during the period on the afternoon of 4 June, when Lieutenant Commander Perkins, and the various relief planes were maintaining a reasonably continuous surveillance of the enemy, constantly transmitting positions and "MOs," that certain messages were received which were at the time inexplicable. The first of these was addressed to Commander Patrol Wing Four from Lieutenant Commander Foley at Dutch Harbor who was acting as the advance operations officer of Patrol Wing Four coordinating the operations in the advanced zone. This message quoted one received at Dutch Harbor from Umnak and which purported to ask for "explicit orders for Army and Navy separately to attack." The message was read over the telephone to General Butler, Commanding the 11th Air Force, and orders requested from him for the Army Air Forces at Umnak to attack. A message was immediately sent to Umnak via Dutch Harbor by Patrol Wing Four's radio system directing Army bombardment at Umnak to attack at once. Before this message was acknowledged, another message was received from Lieutenant Commander Foley requesting confirmation by the Commanding General 11th Air Force of the orders he had given the Army Air Corps bombers at Umnak to take off and attack. This message was immediately telephoned to General Butler who requested that an immediate affirmative reply be made which was done.

From later interviews with Navy pilots on Otter Point Field at the time of this occurrence, it appears that a base troops officer had for some reason or other delayed the take off of the torpedo equipped B-26s to attack the force being covered by Lieutenant Commander Perkins on the grounds that he did not have orders to send them. Lieutenant (j.g.) Breeding, who had just returned from a flight, volunteered to get him the necessary orders through the navy radio system. Lieutenant (j.g.) Breeding states that Colonel Foster told him to keep out of it, and to say where he was. However, Mr. Breeding disregarded these orders, went to the Navy communication tent at Umnak, and transmitted the first of the messages to Lieutenant Commander Foley who relayed the message to Commander Patrol Wing Four. Captain Meals, commanding the B-26s, finally took off to attack the carriers west of Umnak. Only Captain Meals and his wing plane contacted the force, the formation having been dispersed on scouting line enroute. Captain Meals and his wing plane attacked with torpedoes as previously described. On the morning of 6 June, 1942, a PBY returning from an overnight patrol in sector 6 reported a radar contact. Upon request for amplification, he reported "negative clouds." This was immediately followed by another contact report in which he reported visual contact with many enemy ships and "ceiling unlimited." 12 minutes later made a "30 minute E.T.A. to Dutch Harbor" signal. This threw the longitude of the contact in doubt as the position he reported for the contact and the position from which he would make a 30 minute report to Dutch Harbor were 120 miles apart. Nothing was heard of this plane by the intercept watch at Kodiak until one hour later when a second 30 minute E.T.A. report was heard. In the meantime, the Army bombers based at Cold Bay had taken off on the first report and headed for the given position. It was assumed, in the absence of any further reports at the time, that this force would be headed east. An explanation for the two E.T.A. reports separated by an hour was found in the fact that it has been Wing doctrine that a pilot reporting a radar contact must, within 15 minutes, make an amplifying report, or a routine report to indicate that he is proceeding on mission. As strict radio silence had been imposed on all PBYs on patrol during this operation (except for actual contact reports), the only "routine" report available to a pilot was the "30 minute E.T.A.report." It was learned later that the pilot making this contact was only recently designated a P.P.C. and was relatively inexperienced.

At 061435, an amplifying report was forwarded to Com-PatWing Four from Dutch Harbor: "2CA8DD latitude 53 80, longitude 73 10, ceiling unlimited." The first report that the formation included carriers was received from Otter Point, where the pilot landed, via Fort Greeley to ComA1Sec to Com-PatWing Four. The report was received at 061962, although the report itself was timed as 061428. At 062258, a report was received from Umnak, forwarded by Dutch Harbor, that the returning pilot had stated in an interview that he had come on [a] formation suddenly out of the fog in [an] area of unlimited ceiling. The existence of these "bubbles" in the existing weather setup was confirmed by the aerologist. The pilot was immediately chased by quickly launched aircraft. He judged the course to have been roughly southeast, and did not have an opportunity to check the speed of the formation. (NB. This young pilot later in the campaign fully redeemed his poor showing on maintaining a contact on this occasion by the manner in which he fully scouted Kiska and Attu, reporting the first information of the enemy's presence in those islands.)

CHAPTER VII

Others Who Served

There were those who served in Alaska before and after the Dutch Harbor attack. Some fought the Japanese off the islands of Attu and Kiska. These are personal accounts as they witnessed or experienced them. Their various duties give a multiplicity of accounts. It must be kept in mind that because of their positions, assignments and orders as they understood them at the time, the accounts may vary from actual events as they were later known. Still each adds to the complete story of the historic event. Current military status in ().

CHARLES H. PETERSEN, CWO-4, USMC

I was part of a Marine Corps advance detachment to establish a naval air station at Dutch Harbor.

We left the Marine base in San Diego by train in June 1940 (?) for Seattle. Upon arriving at Seattle, we marched single file from the railroad station to [a] Sears, Roebuck warehouse.

At Sears, we were fitted out in all the foul weather gear sold to people in Alaska. [This included] Boon dockers, sheepskin coat, gloves and duck skins. The Marine Corps had no such clothing in their supply depots.

We shipped out of Seattle on two ships: the old steam ship *Northwestern* that had been on the Orient run, and a Navy supply ship the USS [could not remember name].

We spent seven days going straight across the Gulf of Alaska to Dutch Harbor, using the *Northwestern* as a floating barracks.

Upon unloading the USS [unnamed ship], [it] returned to the States. Later on [its] sister ship, the USS *Vega* became our supply ship.

While aboard the *Northwestern*, we were caught in a surprise storm without enough steam up to maneuver, and the *Northwestern* was blown up on the beach.

At the time [I was] the only Marine assigned to the Navy boat crew (the Navy assigned four men: one engineer and 3 coxswains). I went over the side of the *Northwestern* with Tiny Daniels into a life boat and hit the beach. We used the life boat as a ferry evacuating the *Northwestern* by pulling the life boat back and forth with lines between a steam winch on the ship and a tractor on the beach.

The *Northwestern* was filled with gravel sitting on the beach, and converted into a civilian workmen's barracks. This is the ship the Japanese claimed to have sunk.

The shipwreck was on one Saturday, and the following Saturday there was a fire in our supply area and an explosion resulted. I was the only one hurt when something hit me in the head. [The result was] my hair was cut and my head sewed up.

The naval air station was commissioned on Labor Day 1941.

The base now being in an official capacity, and being part of the boat crew, I had the honor of escorting a few girls who had established a business on a small island between Dutch Harbor and Unalaska to a ship bound for the States.

About June 1941, [Alaska Defense Commander Major General Simon Bolivar] Buckner [Jr.] started sending some Army troops in. Just before the troops coming in we had one Army PFC with us. None of us, including the Army PFC, knew what he was supposed to do.

I [also] knew and worked for Bill "Blackie" and Mom Floyd who owned and ran the only bar in Unalaska. After the war, "Blackie" became the National Commander of the Regular Veterans Organization in Washington, DC.

Charles G. Goodwin, Tech 4th Grade, U.S. Army, Radio Operator

I was in Headquarters Company, Third Infantry. We were in the Aleutians when war was declared and I stayed there until the Attu and Kiska campaigns were over in 1943.

Most of my time was spent on outposts around Dutch Harbor. We had one at Makushin on Unalaska, Fisherman's Point on Unalaska and Sedanka Island. We rotated our operators at about one month on each outpost and one month at the net control stations at Fort Mears on Unalaska (a mile from Dutch Harbor docks). Our duties were to observe for any activities, report planes, and make weather reports. There were four men at each outpost: two radiomen and two intelligence men.

A memorable incident for me was just before the invasion of Attu by the enemy, I was in charge of the outpost at Makushin. Suddenly warships were sailing into Makushin Bay—about 258 of them. Visibility wasn't so good and neither I nor the intelligence man from Kentucky could tell if they were friendly. I got on the manual coder (all messages were sent by Morse code) and using as few words as possible, sent in a message to report the armada.

A boat from one of the ships started in and as they grew closer I could see an officer standing up in the boat and he was white, so I was relieved. When he got into shouting distance he yelled, "Don't use your radio so much!" I guess they didn't want our signals to give away their position. The next morning they were gone. This incident was re-told in *The Thousand-Mile War* [Brian Garfield, author].

At the time of the battles my outfit went to Adak where we stayed until the fighting was over.

GEORGE G. MOFFATT, ENSIGN, USS *WATERS* DD115

At the time, I was a junior officer on board the USS *Waters*, DD115. On completing our voyage from Seattle to Chernofski Bay (on the west end of Unalaska Island) during which we had escorted the SS *Delrof* (an Army transport), we were directed to investigate an RDF—Radio Direction Finder fix—and then to proceed to Dutch Harbor for fueling.

Thus, after steaming all night we were in the middle of the Bering Sea, starting an expanding search for what we believed to be an enemy submarine. I don't remember the exact location—probably 100 miles north of Adak Island—when we learned that Dutch Harbor had been attacked, and the fuel dumps set on fire. Evidently the enemy "submarine" we were looking for, was actually the main Japanese attack force. We had crossed paths during the night. This was before radar, so it could have been very close. It was later believed that the attack force had approached from the Bering Sea and passed through Segaum Pass to a position to the south of the Aleutian Islands for the attack on Dutch Harbor.

The USS *Waters* was in a very uncomfortable position: a superior enemy force between us and our base, low on fuel and Dutch Harbor's supplies on fire. Thus the captain, Lieutenant Commander H. J. Armstrong, decided to return to Chernofski and attempt to fuel from the SS D*elrof*. The nervous crew was also assured by the captain that, if necessary, we had enough fuel to reach Kamchatka, peninsula, USSR. But we all knew that this was at economical speed. At any rate, our return to Chernofski was uneventful and for about [the] first time we appreciated the miserable weather with its low visibility.

The Merchant Marine captain aboard the SS *Delrof* was glad to see us return safely, and proceeded to supply us with a full load of fuel oil. By radio our captain informed the Area Commander of his action and status. Very soon after fueling, the *Waters* received orders to proceed to Makushin Bay and report to the OTC (Officer in Tactical Command). Makushin Bay, as I remember it, has a narrow entrance into a bulb-shaped area where ships can anchor near the mountainous area on the north side and be hidden from view from the seaward approaches. Also, the distance to Dutch Harbor by land from Makushin Bay was very close—20 to 25 miles—by sea going around a headland, it was about three times longer.

On arrival to the entrance to Makushin Bay our sonar gear detected a submarine, but the captain told the watch personnel to ignore it as the contact was a USN submarine on picket duty guarding the entrance to the bay, and to give warning should any Japanese ships approach. We entered and found about five other destroyers there. Our captain boated to the ship with the OTC for orders. All the ships present were destroyers, the majority—the older types like our ship—all had fueled somehow. One ship [fueled] from 50 gallon barrels at an old whaling station. The total ships present never exceeded seven, as near as I can remember.

These were the instructions and plans for action to repel any enemy amphibious landing attempt:

First of all, as we were the only Navy force immediately available to defend Dutch Harbor, we should remain concealed until the proper moment and then burst forth to engage and scatter his [the Japanese] amphibious landing boats. Thus, anchor at short-stay close to the land mass, engines to remain on stand-by, no further boating, no signaling by flashing light (use semaphore or flag hoists) and no antiaircraft gunfire unless attacked. The plan of action was to arrive and engage the enemy as the second or third boat wave was landing, torpedoes and gunfire for the ships, plow through the boat waves machine gunning with the rear ships dropping depth charges on shallow setting, all at maximum speed, and then run the gauntlet to enter Dutch Harbor.

The OTC estimated that only two ships at most would reach Dutch Harbor. Because disabling damage was expected, all ships were ordered to prepare for, and hold drills for, repelling boarders; also to be ready to scuttle ships on short notice. (I find it hard to believe at this late date that I actually participated in a repel boarders drill.)

We held our drills and sort of held our breath for a couple of days and nothing much happened. We did see some planes at a distance, briefly, that appeared to be dive bombing Dutch Harbor, but that was all.

OTIS W. BOISE, LIEUTENANT, PLATOON LEADER, I CO., 3RD BN., 37TH INF. REGT. (LIEUTENANT COLONEL, RETIRED)

The regiment was composed of officers and enlisted men selected from various units of the 7th Division stationed along the West Coast. Organizing the battalion was accomplished at Camp Murray, Washington, a part of the Fort Lewis reservation, and proved to be frustrating and depressing to many of us. But in time we were organized well enough to resemble a military unit.

Late in May 1942, we boarded the *President Fillmore* which was docked at Seattle. But our departure was delayed for 24 hours while additional munitions including artillery shells, small arms ammunition, explosives, torpedoes and mustard gas were loaded aboard. We finally departed Puget Sound late in the afternoon expecting to take the inland passage, but the Japanese task force headed toward the Aleutian Islands had been sighted and the decision was made to get us to Unalaska as fast as possible. So we took the direct route across the Gulf [of Alaska], the first merchant vessel to do so since the start of the war. We arrived late in the evening of June 2, and as we approached the inlet to the harbor we began to receive semaphore messages from a signal unit ashore asking the captain to identify the ship and to give the password.

There was a great deal of confusion because our signal people were not responding correctly and to make matters worse, our naval escort had moved to the port side of our ship standing broadside to shore and mysteriously a submarine was now following us with its conning tower above water. (Fortunately this was a friendly submarine that apparently sighted us as we approached the inlet to the harbor and was giving us a close look.) This had all the earmarks of an enemy task force, so an artillery battery commander at a gun position near the inlet of the harbor, was given an order to fire a warning round over the bow of the ship, and that is exactly what he did!

There was a terrific explosion as the round exploded in the water just short of the bow. You can imagine the havoc this created aboard the ship. The captain immediately put the ship in full reverse to stop our forward movement and the crew quickly raised flags on the masts to identify us. About this time a Kingfisher scout plane approached us from shore, made several circles around us and went back to shore. Fortunately the shore [batteries] were friendly and signaled we could proceed to dock. This confusion apparently resulted from the fact that the people at Dutch Harbor were not informed that our ship was to take a direct route across the Gulf, thereby arriving several days ahead of schedule, and likewise the ship's officers were not in possession of the correct password.

We anchored in the harbor for a considerable time while docking procedures were arranged so that it was well after dark before the ship tied up to the dock. The *Fillmore* was the largest ship to have docked at Dutch Harbor and because of its size, along with high tide, the main deck was at least one deck above the dock level. A large group of people had gathered on the dock, including the port commander, who asked to speak to the commander of troops. This was Lieutenant Colonel Swenson who was at the deck rail along with many of the rest of us. The colonel identified himself and the port commander instructed Swenson to get the troops off the ship as quickly as possible. Swenson suggested it would be better to disembark during daylight hours, but the port commander insisted we get off the ship *now.*

Because the main deck was so far above the dock, gang planks could not reach the main deck so they were placed at two small gangways below the main deck. These gangways were not much wider than the width of an average man and became a real bottleneck, especially since each man had to carry a barracks bag, gun, gas mask, etc. The dock was under semi-blackout condition making identification of individual people difficult. So the troops were assembled on the dock in about platoon size groups and were escorted off the dock and toward town by guides. Since these groups were a mixture of several companies, we officers had little or no command responsibilities so we fell in alongside the groups and followed the guides.

As I recall, the road from the dock to town was perhaps two to three miles long and of course was rough, muddy, and there was virtually no light. In time we arrived at the cable drawn ferry, crossed the channel and then on to town were the troops were led to housing of some sort. (I never did learn where they spent the night.) The officers were led to two Quonset huts placed end-to-end perpendicular to and within a few yards of the main road. Army cots had been placed along both walls of the hut and each officer selected a cot and began preparing for bed. A major wearing a parka, wool head gear with the ear covers tied at the top of the cap and a major's leaf pinned in front entered the door accompanied by a first lieutenant. He introduced himself and said he was from the 1st Battalion. In essence he said: "I don't know how much you have been told, but we are expecting an air raid sometime between the third and fifth, and an invasion of the island soon after, so tomorrow morning at around six o'clock if you hear antiaircraft fire, that is not reveille but an air raid! Get out of this building and seek cover. Do your men have ammunition?"

We had not been issued ammunition and he was told this, so he turned to the lieutenant and told him to get enough cases to leave one case at each place where our troops were located. He spoke briefly with some of the officers and then left. This was the first indication we had that the Japanese were approaching the islands and it was difficult for most of us to comprehend this and we went to bed not fully realizing what lay ahead.

This might be a good time to briefly bring out how ill prepared we were to be entering a theater of operation. When we left Seattle, we didn't even know we were heading to Alaska. There had been much speculation, and rumors were running wild with many thinking we would sail for the South Pacific and others that we would sail for Alaska. We had not been issued boots, cold weather clothing or equipment, so it was difficult to believe we would be going to Alaska, but the strongest rumors had us going there. It wasn't until we were out of sight of land that an announcement came over the loud speakers that indeed Dutch Harbor was our destination. When we disembarked, we were in Class A uniforms (pinks, blouses and leggings for the officers, World War I helmets and gas masks). The enlisted men also had World War I helmets and gas masks and not all of them carried the new M-1 rifle.

At almost exactly 6 a.m., on the morning of the third [of June] (as predicted by the major the night before), we were jolted out of bed by antiaircraft fire and other explosions. We hurriedly dressed and dashed out the door. To the rear of the building, a ditch about four feet deep and about two feet wide had been dug perpendicular to the building which I suspect was to be used for a water line, and it was this ditch that we jumped into. I used the word jumped because that is exactly what we did and my aim was not so good because I landed directly on top of Colonel Methvin (correct spelling of name unknown), the regimental commander! He turned to me and said, "Good morning lieutenant." I was so flustered I don't remember apologizing!

From our vantage point we could see the Japanese bomber formation flying above Fort Mears and the harbor with strings of bombs falling from the planes and their Zeros making strafing runs. Even though we were two or three miles away from this enemy action, we viewed this with a good deal of disbelief and apprehension fearing that the attack would shift our way. Our fears were well founded because a Zero came roaring over the mountains to the south, dropped down to tree-top level and strafed the road in front of us. As the planed passed, we could see the flash of gun fire from the nose of the plane as well as the pilot in the cockpit. At least two of the officers in the ditch had rifles and they were able to get off a couple [of] rounds or so before the plane was gone. Had the pilot noticed us in the ditch in time to swing the plane in line with it, I'm confident he would have inflicted several casualties among us.

By now we could see smoke from fires in and around the harbor and we also realized the planes were gone and the raid was over for the time being. There was a great deal of confusion as could be expected. Many of the troops as well as officers had gathered in small groups watching the fires and discussing the raid. Some of the men had fled to the nearby hills and I recall two officers headed toward the harbor commenting they wanted to see "how much damage had been inflicted".

Very shortly, orders came down that we were to gather up our gear as quickly as possible and move up Unalaska Valley. As the men gathered with their gear, the officers would form them up into small groups and head up the valley, and as I recall, the march was about two miles long. This was our assigned area, and some tentage had been erected, but it was several days before all personnel were in tents.

Sometime after noon, the battalion commander held an officers' call at which time he gave us a little more information of the existing situation and said one platoon of I Company would relieve a platoon of the 2nd Battalion occupying an outpost at Ugadaga Gap, and a reconnaissance of the area would be made that afternoon. As soon as the meeting was over, my company commander turned to me and said my platoon would be the one to occupy the outpost and that he and I and one other officer would leave immediately to make the reconnaissance.

We completed that task and were about half way back to the cantonment area when the air raid alarm sounded and within a very short time the second Japanese raid was under way. I guess you could say we had ring side seats because from our location we could look down on much of the town and the harbor and watch the destruction taking place. Some of the flight formations flew directly over us, but we were quite confident that the enemy wouldn't waste ammunition on three soldiers sitting on the side of a hill!

My platoon occupied the outpost on the fifth [of June] and we made preparation for the invasion that happily never came. However, on two different occasions during our first week of occupation, my sentries detected [people] coming up the trail from Ugadaga Bay toward our outpost. They were short and carried huge packs on their backs. As a precaution I stationed two or three men with rifles on each side of the trail and waited for them to arrive. Seeing that they were unarmed, I met them and asked who they were were and where they were going. They said they were Aleuts and had fled the town after the first raid and that they were now on their way back home.

JAMES G. SMALL, COMMANDER, BATTERY G 260TH CA (AA)
(CAPTAIN, U.S. ARMY RET.)

We arrived at Dutch Harbor [aboard the *President Fillmore* from Fort Lawton, Washington] about 9 p.m. June 2, 1942. In this latitude at this time of year, it was still daylight. Dutch Harbor was not Battery G's destination, but the ship stopped there to discharge the 3rd Battalion, 37th Infantry (which had several soldiers killed in the raid nine hours later), and to unload cargo that was to be delivered at that station.

About 6 a.m., June 3, General Quarters was sounded. This was our initiation into enemy activity. The battery responded as well trained troops should: by reporting immediately to their assigned stations. The ship itself was cast off from the dock and cleared the dock area into the harbor.

Over their Dutch Harbor target, the Japanese were blessed with clear skies and a 10,000 foot ceiling. They made their attack with 14 bombers and three fighters which had been launched from the carrier *Ryujo*. (The carrier *Junyo* also launched planes for this raid, but, due to navigational problems, their planes did not proceed to Dutch Harbor, but returned to the *Junyo*.)

The attacking force was over Dutch Harbor for about 20 minutes during which time they bombed the tank farms, the radio station, the barracks and strafed the ships and Navy PBYs in the harbor. An extremely intense retaliatory fire was put up by the guns of Battery G against every plane that came into their range. Most of the targets during this raid were ideal for three-inch AA guns since they were in their range and flew their bomb runs in a straight and level pattern. After the initial raid, there were quite a few General Quarters alerts which proved to be false alarms. However, each General Quarters necessitated that someone on shore had to cast off the ship tied to the dock.

The harbor master Commander Carl "Squeaky" Anderson had supervised the difficult task of building a dock at Dutch Harbor which required some masterful engineering for the dock was anchored to rock which dropped precipitously into the sea. How it was anchored there is beyond my comprehension, but it was done under his supervision and a fine dock had been completed shortly before our arrival. Understandably, the commander was very proud of his dock, but I thought his comments during one of the many false alerts was almost heartless when he yelled: "Get that —— ship out of here, I don't want my dock blown up!"

During another General Quarters alarm, the civilian workers who were helping to unload the *Fillmore* took off for the hills as soon as the klaxon sounded. A brigadier general was on the pier in his Jeep and saw the men scattering. He yelled for them to come back and cast the ship off from the dock. They kept running away and the general called to them again. They disregarded his calls again so he stood up in the Jeep and fired one round from his .45 pistol over their heads and yelled once more for them to come back. They did and, thus freed, we sailed into the harbor.

During lulls between raids and false alerts, crews unloaded the cargo assigned to that station. At night, destroyers and submarines tied up along side the ship and fuel was transferred to them so they could continue their patrols.

One June 4, we experienced quite a few more false alerts, but at 5:50 p.m. we underwent a second attack. The carriers *Ryujo* and *Junyo* launched 11 dive bombers, six high level bombers and 15 fighters against Dutch Harbor. Evidently the Japanese had photos from their raid of the previous day and had selected particular targets for this mission. Among the targets hit were one end of the hospital, four fuel tanks were destroyed, one 37mm AA gun emplacement was hit, the ship *Northwestern* was badly damaged by bombs and fire. (It is thought by some this ship was mistaken for the *Fillmore* which had given them so much trouble the day before.)

The *Fillmore* was away from the dock and in the harbor during this attack. Several fighters made hostile passes at us and we reacted with as much firepower as we could against every target presented. Due to the fjord nature of that country, it was difficult to assess which targets were hit because they passed behind a peak or mountain before your effectiveness could be determined. However, several of these attacking planes emitted smoke and flew erratically after passing through our fire.

I feel that, due to my experience with the men of the battery, that they were capable men who reacted calmly to their mission and must have been effective. A Japanese Zero crashed on an adjacent island with a .50 caliber hole through its fuel line [later investigation revealed it was the oil line]. Even though the Navy claims they shot this plane down, I believe that it may have been hit by G Battery because it had been in our area, we had fired at such a target and, further, we were one of the few units which had fired at such a target with a .50 caliber AA machine gun. This particular Zero was recovered and shipped to the U.S. where it was flown, studied and evaluated. [This was] the first such plane we were able to use for such purposes.

Even though there were no more attacks by the Japanese, we did have three or four false alerts for the next several days. Crews continued to unload cargo over the next few days.

On June 6, about 40 wounded and most of the civilian population were evacuated from Dutch Harbor by the *Fillmore*. The ship finally sailed to Cold Bay where Battery G was unloaded, our assigned post being Fort Randall which was located there. We set up an AW AA defense around the air strip at that station. Shortly after our settling in, we received orders that we were to be transferred to Fort Morrow, Alaska (at Port Heiden) upon arrival of the 203rd C.A. AA Regiment. This regiment soon came in and freed us to go on to our next assignment. We proceeded to Fort Morrow on board the Moore-McCormack Lines Victory Ship *MorMacSea*. After unloading, we set up the AW AA defense of this post. Our armament was supplemented by the addition of eight Oerlikon AA guns on Navy pedestal mounts.

I found [the American soldier] to be proud to do his assigned task. He is courageous despite danger. He will respond quickly and properly to combat situations. He is adaptable to changing situations in a rational and intelligent way without constant direct supervision.

I am thankful that no one in this unit was wounded or killed in this action.

It was an honor to command such a unit.

CHAPTER VIII

The Aleutian Campaign Begins

The Dutch Harbor attack was the beginning of a 14-month struggle. The Japanese occupied Kiska and Attu. They had photographed Adak and went ashore briefly on Amchitka. In spite of their presence on these barren islands, Japanese interest in the Aleutians was not to gain and hold more territory. For sure, their efforts in the South Pacific were more in keeping with conquest and territorial accumulation. When the Midway strike began to falter with signs of defeat, Admiral Yamamoto called off further intrusion into the Aleutians. But it was too late to withdraw committed troops and equipment. From this it might be assumed the Aleutian campaign was indeed a diversionary effort by the Japanese. Evidence points to the fact there was never a strong desire to hold the Aleutians as additional Japanese island territory.

No matter. The die had been cast with the attack on Dutch Harbor. Three days later, 2,500 well trained Japanese soldiers landed on Kiska and Attu. By June 10, when no weather reports had been received from these distant weather stations, American forces were alerted. A counter attack and invasion of the islands would begin.

American efforts to reclaim the Aleutian territory from the Japanese involved the invasion of Attu and the bombardment of Kiska. The battle for these extreme western islands in the Aleutian Chain was only the beginning of an arduous struggle in continually inhospitable conditions.

In April 1943, a bloody recapture of Attu succeeded. On August 15, 1943, American troops invaded Kiska in an attempt to reclaim it. But the Japanese had evacuated en masse in late July using two light cruisers and ten destroyers. They left without a struggle and the ever present fog covered their leaving as quietly as when they arrived.

The war in the north had come to an end. But the battle with the weather continued. Bases were completed, supplies were ferried in, men and equipment struggled to keep from freezing, and air strikes were made against the Kurile Islands of Japan.

Few Americans in the Lower 48 knew much about the Aleutian Campaign. It was not as spectacular as the battles waged in the South Pacific with its exotic island names that have become hallmarks of island warfare. The heroism, struggle and sacrifices made in the Aleutians did not get as much front page play. Yet the combination of unrelenting weather and extremes of cold, wind and sea were equally troublesome as on any other war front.

Flying the lumbering PBYs on patrol and in battle, air crews were stretched to their limits of physical and emotional endurance. Ground crews and other military forces used their ingenuity to keep themselves and their equipment ready. Sometimes communications faltered, signals were misinterpreted, or even incorrect. Frequently command responsibilities were confused. Yet the Aleutians were held and the invaders left, having experienced their own frustration with trying to fight a war where they should not have been.

****

C. P. BROOKE, 250TH COAST ARTILLERY

I was a doctor at Dutch Harbor in 1943, temporarily attached to the 250th Coast Artillery. Our biggest problem after the Japanese were expelled from the Aleutians was having something to do. Most of the hospital cases were the normal ailments, accidents, skin diseases from the cold and damp and some self-inflicted wounds.

An artilleryman came in one day to get a routine circumcision, partially out of boredom and partially because of health reasons. The operation, although minor in nature, does immobilize the patient for a number of days.

Word got out to other platoons and soon I was performing three to four operations a day. I was happy to get the surgical practice and it relieved boredom on my part too.

During this period when so many men were in the hospital, the commanding officer of the artillery unit called for a trial alert to test his defenses. Some of the guns could not be manned properly because so many men were immobilized.

Needless to say, the commanding officer was very upset and orders were issued that only one man from a platoon could be circumcised at a time.

Pill boxes used by American defenders during the attack. These and five others are in front of the new luxury hotel, the Grand Aleutian.
Photo Courtesy Patricia Brown Darling, Akutan, Alaska

FOR VICTORY
Buy United States
Bonds Stamps

SERVE IN SILENCE
Do Not Reveal
Military Information

Anchorage Daily Times

READ BY ALASKANS EVERYWHERE

TWENTY-SIXTH YEAR　　ANCHORAGE, ALASKA, FRIDAY, JUNE 5, 1942　　PRICE TEN CENTS

HUGE SEA FIGHT RAGES

Report Heavy Losses To Jap Fleet At Midway Island

Order All Stop Lights On Cars Blacked Out

Rigid Enforcement For 11 To 2 Dark Period Decreed By Officials

In redoubling efforts toward enforcement of total blackout in Anchorage, civilian defense officials and city police announced today that violators of blackout regulations are subject to arrest and trial.

B. C. Raynor, civilian defense director, issued a warning today to motorists driving during the blackout period from 11 p. m. to 2 a. m. Tail lights on all cars must either be blacked out with a dimming tape, painted black or disconnected. Headlights, of course, are banned and use of blue or other colored paper to dim them is prohibited.

Total blackout between 11 p. m. and 2 a. m. in Anchorage and vicinity will continue indefinitely, Raynor announced on orders of Fort Richardson.

Observations made by authorities during last night's blackout proved that the rear red lights on automobiles are a definite hazard and should be completely darkened by either of the methods suggested.

Four arrests were made by city police last night for hindering enforcement of emergency regulations.

William E. Struve was arrested at Fifth avenue and C street for being drunk and disorderly and fighting with arresting officers, the police blotter shows. Struve was fined $20 by City Magistrate Karl Drager this morning and sentenced to five days in jail. Three automobiles were apprehended for blackout violations.

Drivers are warned by officials that they are subject to arrest if found driving about the city during emergencies unless on official business. Cab drivers are requested to stand by their cars for call by those authorized to use such transportation.

Study Election Plan For Naming Alaska Governors

WASHINGTON, D. C., June 5. (AP)—The proposal to permit of governors in Alaska, Hawaii and Puerto Rico as a step toward local self-government was urged today by the Foreign Policy Association in a study prepared for private research by Charles F. Reid, a staff member.

The report also declared consideration should be given for statehood for those territories.

Berlin Admits 8,000 Killed In Two Cities

SILHOUETTES OF THE MIKADO'S WAR PLANES

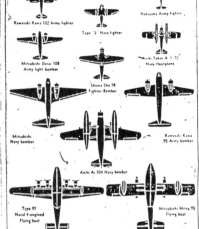

Kawasaki Kawa 102 Army fighter
Nakajima Army fighter
Type '5' Navy fighter
Mitsubishi Dazai 108 Army light bomber
Aichi Tokei A 1 '92' Navy floatplane
Showa Sho 98 Fighter-Bomber
Mitsubishi Navy bomber
Kawasaki Kawa 95 Army bomber
Aichi As 104 Navy bomber
Type 97 Naval 4-engined Flying boat
Mitsubishi Mitsu 95 Flying boat

BRITISH DESERT ARMY HOLDS GERMANS AT BAY

By Associated Press

General Rommel, leader of the Nazi Benefit forces, was reported today to be moving strong reinforcements in the bloody 11-day battle of North Africa as the British announced they had smashed an axis tank assault at Bir El Hacheim after the German demands to surrender the key stronghold.

That desert water hole is the southern anchor for the 50-mile British line stretched across the hot sands to the Mediterranean.

British headquarters said Indian troops struck in the rear to relieve the Free French garrison at Bir El Hacheim after the defenders twice rejected the German demands to surrender the key stronghold.

Other European war developments told of two blows against Germany's northern battlefront. London said RAF bombers scored direct hits on a 35,000-ton German battleship and the heavy cruiser Admiral Hipper. The attack was carried out at Trondheim where the ships are berthed.

Soviet dispatches reported Russian planes were fighting to safeguard the ocean route around the top of Norway and hammered home three sharp attacks on bases from which German planes were attacking the convoys.

At least 48 Nazi planes were reported destroyed and Nazi airfields were heavily damaged by these raids.

Reports Oil At Indian

P. R. Strong Exhibits Bottle of Liquid

Peter H. Strong, 83, who has been developing a mine near Indian for the past 40 years and claims to have ore containing a million dollars' worth of gold copper and oil on his property.

Mr. Strong brought two quarts of his product to town and requests that a pipeline only 28 miles long could be installed to supply the city with all its petroleum needs.

The old-timer whose mine is on the north shore of Turnagain Arm, said he has a half acre of ground saturated with oil. He wheeled out 1,000 wheelbarrow loads of dirt and drained off the oil, he said.

"Mr. Strong said development of his mine has been delayed by the need of a mill to take the gold out of the quartz rock. He said it runs two cents to the ton, or about $70.

Nelson Names Secy. Wickard Foods Chief

WASHINGTON, D. C., June 5. (AP)—War Production Board Chairman Donald M. Nelson today named Secretary of Agriculture Claude R. Wickard as food requirements chief.

Pacific Coast Radio Stations Off The Air

SAN FRANCISCO, June 5. (AP)—All Pacific coast radio stations went off the air last night in accordance with orders issued by the Western Defense Command and the Fourth Army last night.

Land Largest Convoy In India

NEW DELHI, June 5. (AP)—

Cancel Plans For Building Water System

Lack of Shipping Space Given As Reason For Project's End

All registration work on the $65,000 gravity water system and water distribution project for Anchorage and vicinity has been called off and efforts have been made to stop the work, it was learned today, according to Mayor William F. Stolt and H. Hufman, contractor for the distribution system.

Lack of shipping facilities for transport of materials was given as reason for the order to stop work.

Preliminary surveys have been completed by Hufman for the city distribution system and the contract for the gravity line has also yet been let.

More than a year ago had the gravity line installation to the upper Ship Creek area was to have cost $26,000 include the storage tank and would have supplied water to city mains. But this would still be filled with water to have been mixed and explored with new pipe.

The city distribution system was to have cost $65,000 provided by the Federal Works Agency.

Plans are underway by the city to build a sump in the city bowl for collection of water for fire fighting purposes. The sump would be filled by springs and filled to the level of the business and residential districts by a pump.

Present of Fourth avenue from the present paving ending at C street to the railroad tracks for Fourth avenue has been approved by the Works Agency but in all probability will not be put through," according to Mayor Stolt. The improvement is not likely that the paving project will be developed.

Blast Wrecks Huge Arsenal

JOLIET, Ill., June 5. (AP)—An explosion that "rocked" the mammoth Elwood Arsenal, one of the largest in the nation, leaving at least 21 dead, was announced today by Captain Tim Stall, Army press relations officer.

He said more than 5 score were injured but 28 others working a nearby shipping building received minor injuries.

The blast was heard as far as 50 miles away and occurred at 2:45 a. m. It destroyed one shipping-building and the entire shell-loading plant which was described by the director as the largest in the world. The Tumult section which was blown out was a loading section.

Seattle Morale High Despite Dutch Harbor

SEATTLE, June 5. (AP)—This principal Pacific Northwest city greeted the end of fears against attack on Japanese bases and Alaska Way as main waterfront directed to petroleum and motor traffic following the imposition of drastic new waterfront restrictions.

Air raid wardens and officials scheduled dozens of business plots and instruction personnel.

Stephen Chadwick, former National commander of the American Legion, termed a full-scale air raid drill shortly after the Civilian War Council placed Seattle's morale high after the Dutch Harbor attack and rumor-mongering was increasing.

Navy Orders Tighter Ban On Night Spots

LOS ANGELES, June 5. (AP)—Hollywood and Los Angeles cafes and night clubs selling liquor must keep prostitutes from spot-questionable women and attack either in or declared an all bounds.

Lieut. Comdr. C. H. Fogg, commanding the Navy's shore patrol, said a new area gave the navy the power to a meeting called by the southern California tavern association.

The situation in Los Angeles and Hollywood has become so serious we have had to increase our shore patrol per cent, he said.

"We have one example of a merchant marine man discharged in a Los Angeles night spot sector plans for the sailing of a convoy.

"We have other examples of attempts to get information from service men by plying them with liquor in bars.

"Remember," liquor and tongues and a careless word may endanger a ship, or even an entire convoy.

"We expect you to protect service men from prostitutes who spread disease, apart from drunk rollers. We expect you to refuse to serve drinks to navy service men who may be slightly intoxicated."

Ray Adams, tavern association manager, said that "we know the enemy has a spy at secrecy in Los Angeles that gives no help. All lines of information against "agents from service men is retaining in kind and then measured.

"If you want an ace of anti-liberals, then you will have to cut charming and tolerance toward women, you know are prostitutes."

U.S. Defenders Fight Off Air, Sea Attacks

Military Observers See It As Crucial Point In Pacific's Control

WASHINGTON, D. C., June 5. (AP)—Navy and Japanese fleet units were apparently engaged today in one of the greatest battles of the Pacific as the result of the enemy's attempt all-out bid yesterday to end the strong garrisoned United States outpost at Midway Island.

Commenting on a communique issued at Pearl Harbor by Admiral Nimitz commander of the Pacific fleet, naval experts here emphasized the point that Nimitz said the "attack was continuing." This seemed to indicate, they said, that the fight had continued for many hours.

Both the American and enemy units were said to be maneuvering for an advantage in what may be a crucial engagement to determine the enemy's ability to strike at more vital points including Pearl Harbor, the United States West Coast, Alaska and even the Panama Canal.

Earlier communiques reported American battle forces slashing anew at a powerful Japanese naval squadron off Midway Island after bearing off a dawn attack at 6:35 a. m. yesterday. The foray was described by Admiral Nimitz as the heaviest raid on that six-times-attacked island since December 7.

The enemy force included battleships, aircraft "carriers and cruisers. Losses to the enemy were said to be heavy.

"Our attacks are continuing to serve the enemy," Admiral Nimitz's headquarters said.

Meanwhile, President Roosevelt declared authoritative reports had been received that Japs were using poison gas in the war with China and the United States would retaliate "in kind and in" proportion.

GUS JOHNSON PASSES AWAY

U.S. FLEET IN PURSUIT OF JAPS

FOR VICTORY Buy UNITED STATES WAR BONDS & STAMPS

Anchorage Daily Times

"READ BY ALASKANS EVERYWHERE"

SERVE IN SILENCE
Do Not Reveal
Military Information

TWENTY-SIXTH YEAR — ANCHORAGE, ALASKA, SATURDAY, JUNE 6, 1942 — PRICE TEN CENTS

HIT AT LEAST EIGHT SHIPS

DEEP IN EMBATTLED CHINA

CREMATION IN CHANGSHA left this blot on the Chinese city. Japanese burned their fallen comrades because that is their custom and because it conceals extent of Jap casualties, which ran to many thousands in this epic Chinese victory. Returning Chinese troops and civilians are shown.

DESERTED CITY was Changsha as Japanese approached. This is one of the main streets in the city of 300,000 as it appeared after evacuation ordered by Chinese Gen. Hsueh Yueh. Not many days later the street once again teemed—following hurried departure of the enemy.

British Send 1,300 Planes Over Europe

LONDON, June 6. (AP)—The RAF [illegible] off a week which saw the opening of the greatest air offensive in history with the third [illegible] night assault on the German Ruhr [illegible] night.

The British also [illegible] what observers called the [illegible] of the week against the [illegible] coastline of France in a daylight attack which meant that probably more than 1,000 planes, fighters and bombers, [illegible] out across the English channel for various Nazi targets.

Possibly 300 were out in the night raid, the air ministry disclosed.

It was also announced that observation planes had established the fact that about eight square miles of Cologne had been devastated during the week of raiding and that "the greater part of the old town of Cologne is finished."

Sentence Two Americans

WASHINGTON, D. C., June 6. (AP)—Two American and one Japanese were sentenced to prison today for violating the Foreign Agents' Registration law.

It was the first case of its kind tried thus far in which Jap agents were involved with Americans.

The latter were Frederick Vincent Williams and David Warren Ryder both of San Francisco, and Tsutomu Obana, secretary of the Japanese Chamber of Commerce of San Francisco.

The Americans received sentences of 16 months in jail and the Japanese two to six months.

American Flying Tigers Attack, Kill Japanese

CHUNGKING, June 6. (AP)—The Flying Tigers of the American Volunteer Group killed more than 200 Japanese soldiers yesterday along the west bank of the Salween river which the Burma road parallels for some distance, it was officially announced today.

During May the AVG shot down 24 enemy pursuit planes and destroyed 35 on the ground.

The Americans lost six planes and five pilots.

Promise Sales Tax If Big Bill Goes Through

WASHINGTON, D. C., June 6. (AP)—The house ways and means committee was reported today to have put the administration on notice formally that the tax goal of $8,700,000,000 could not to be achieved without a federal sales tax.

Informed sources said Chairman Doughton and other leaders told Secretary Morgenthau they could not write a bill of that size without over riding to some extent his opposition to a direct consumer [illegible]

WAR BRIEFS From Many Points

WASHINGTON, D. C., June 6. (AP)—At least eight Japanese warships and transports including possibly two aircraft carriers suffered severe damage in a mighty sea fight with U. S. fleet units off Midway Island, Navy department communiques said today.

TOKYO, June 6. (AP)—The Japanese command in central China announced today the city of Chuhsien in Chekiang province was occupied at [illegible] day.

Domei said the city is the key [illegible] point for China's east coast.

NEW YORK, June 6. (AP)—The Berlin radio said today that the Soviet naval base at Sevastopol was attacked by extremely heavy artillery fire from an "encircling front."

NEW YORK, June 6. (AP)—Berlin announced today that German submarines have sunk 15 enemy vessels totaling 108,000 tons in the Western Atlantic and Caribbean Sea.

ALLIED HEADQUARTERS, Australia, June 6. (AP)—Warehouses, docks and coaling jetties at the Japanese-occupied base of Rabaul, New Britain, were bombed again last night by allied warplanes, General MacArthur's headquarters announced today.

Axis Accounts For Another 6

By Associated Press

Two more United Nations' ships were torpedoed in the Atlantic, the Navy disclosed today, bringing the announced losses there in two days to six merchant vessels.

A Navy patrol boat landed with two teen-age survivors of the latest sinkings who said their Norwegian ship was torpedoed in the Atlantic on May 21. They spent five days in an open boat until they were sighted by a Dutch merchantman. Twenty-four hours later the Dutch ship met a similar fate and the boys spent three more days in a lifeboat before being picked up by the patrol plane.

Only 14 of the original 40 on the Norwegian ship survived, the boys said. Fifteen Chinese crewmen were killed on the Dutch ship.

Explosion Fails To Halt Work

JOLIET, Ill., June 6. (AP)—Munitions rolled off the Elwood ordnance plant lines in volume today while Army officials attempted to identify all 51 persons dead and missing in the thunderous blast yesterday.

Officials said the explosion in the world's largest shell-loading plant wrecked only one of twelve units of the vast works and the other loading lines calmly continued on a 24-hour basis [illegible]

Attacking Sub Believed Sunk

[illegible]

PLANE CARRIER STRUCK BY AIR DEFENDERS; U.S. THWARTS JAP LANDING

HONOLULU, June 6. (AP)—A crushing defeat of the big Japanese fleet which attempted to seize Midway Island in a desperate bid for control of the mid-Pacific, was indicated in official navy communiques today.

The defeat grew in proportions as the United States pressed home new attacks.

The enemy appeared to be limping away.

The situation seemed to presage a victory even greater than the Coral Sea.

"While it is too early to claim a major Jap disaster, it may be conservatively stated that the United States control remains firm in the Midway area," the commander in chief of the Pacific fleet announced last night.

"The enemy appears to be withdrawing but we are continuing to battle."

No actual sinkings were listed in the cryptic accounts of the battle which the Japs opened with the use of warplanes based on carriers last Thursday after what was possibly a feinting attack on Dutch Harbor.

Admiral Nimitz said however, that a Japanese aircraft carrier was hit by aerial defenders in the first stages of the fighting and was later struck by three torpedoes.

"As more reports come in it appears that the damage to the enemy was very heavy indeed," the navy chief declared. "The damage involved several ships in each class—carrier, battleship, cruiser and transport."

This was the first mention of Japanese transports bringing landing support for the other enemy units. It was believed that the huge Japanese forces were risking much for the assault far from their home bases, and had as their goal the actual conquest of Midway Island.

In desperation at the pending defeat, the Japs were reported to have machine-gunned United States fliers who were forced to bail out during dog fights. Americans adrift in rubber boats were believed to have suffered similar treatment.

At least two Jap carriers each with 20 to 30 planes were included in the axis armada but the size and nature of the United States forces were wrapped largely in secrecy beyond the admiral's statement that "the brunt of the defense to date has fallen upon the aviation personnel in which the Army, Navy and Marine Corps were all represented."

Nimitz, returning from a visit to Midway a month ago, voiced praise for his men there.

Admiral Chester Nimitz said the Japanese aircraft carriers, battleships, cruisers and transports were all dealt damaging blows. At least eight warships and transports must have been damaged on the basis of Nimitz's statement.

Rommel Loses 340 Tanks In Desert Beating

LONDON, June 6. (AP)—The German desert army commander, General Rommel, lost 340 tanks, about one-half his armored force in the 12-day battle of Libya, dispatches from the war front said.

This gave the British mechanized superiority as they continued to pound Rommel's spearhead backwards toward the gap in the British lines that the Germans have been fighting desperately to keep open.

A military commentator said Lieut. Gen. Neil Ritchie retained the initiative after driving the Germans out of Tamar west of Kingsbridge.

The attack which developed two nights ago appeared today to have turned into a three-sided onslaught.

To Pledge Revenge Pearl Harbor Day

WASHINGTON, D. C., June 6. (AP)—Exactly six months to the minute after the Japanese dropped their first bombs on Pearl Harbor [illegible] December [illegible] Marines and Coast [illegible]

Three Given 1-A Ratings

Three men were classified 1-A by the Anchorage draft board at its meeting on Thursday. The men were Ted K. Bo[illegible], John H. Ollom and Walter Bentz.

Other classifications follow: 2-A, Clayton D. Webber, Norm[illegible] C. Woodring, Gordon Johns[illegible], James D. Skaggs, Nick D. Gr[illegible]ory, Calvert W. Butler and Cla[illegible] G. Spensley.

Class 3-A, Frederick Br[illegible], Carl A. Johnson, Thomas [illegible]hane, Victor C. Rivers [illegible] Ervien H. Fluegel.

Conferees Agree On $16 Army Pay

WASHINGTON, D. C., June [illegible] (AP)—The senate and house conference committee comprised yesterday on the soldiers' increased pay bill and agreed [illegible] basic minimum [illegible] months [illegible] in the army [illegible]

See Siberia Next On List

CHUNGKING, June 6 (AP)—Lieut. Gen. Stillwell, American commander-in-chief of the Chinese forces that fought the Japs in Burma, arrived here today with Maj. Gen. Brereton, commander of the U. S. Army Air Force in India for conferences with General Chiang Kai-Shek. They were accompanied by Brig. Gen. Chennault, commander of the American Volunteer Group.

Meanwhile, a Chinese spokesman said he heard reports of new Japanese concentrations at Manchukuo but could not give the size of the increase in forces.

The speculation in Chinese circles over the Japanese failure to invade Australia and the failure so far to enter India, gave rise to a firm belief that Soviet Siberia might be the next big Japanese target.

House Votes Out Funds For CCC

WASHINGTON, D. C., June 6. [illegible] recommen[illegible] appropriation com[illegible]

8,000 Japanese Killed In Single Day of Fighting

CHUNGKING, June 6. (AP)—The Chinese command announced today about 8,000 Japs had been killed or wounded yesterday in fighting around Chuhsien, a rail center in western Chekiang.

That increased the Japanese casualties in two days of fighting to 10,000.

Observers here said that the Chinese announcement might indicate a decisive turn in the fierce battle of the western Chekiang air base area which the Japanese might bomb.

Food Storage Plan Awaits Official Word

Preparation of storage space for a supply of food adequate in Anchorage for three months is pending word from Juneau, according to Mayor William A. Stolt.

The offer of the food supply was made by the federal government and Governor Ernest Gruening requested that storage space be provided for it.

Some warehouse room has been obtained, Mayor Stolt said, and it is expected that the word from [illegible] will have more specific [illegible]

Indict Six Powder Firms

PHILADELPHIA, June 6 (AP)—E. I. DuPont and deNemours Company and five other explosive manufacturers were indicted by a federal grand jury late yesterday on charges of conspiring to fix prices in violation of the anti-trust act.

Others named were the Hercules Powder Company, the Atlas Powder Company, Austin Powder Company, Illinois Powder Manufacturing Company, and the King Powder Company.

The indictment contended that the effect of the alleged conspiracy was to "maintain prices on commercial explosives and blasting supplies to all classes of consumers at high arbitrary and artificial levels."

Announce Rites.

Burial services will be held for Lars A. Warberg next Monday evening at 8 o'clock from the Anchorage Funeral Parlors, it was announced today by officials of the American Legion who will conduct the rites.

All former service men who plan to attend were requested to meet at the Pioneer Hall at 7:30 o'clock.

TRIAL CONTINUES

SEATTLE, June 6. (AP)—Retrial of Edward [illegible] Yager for the [illegible]

FOR VICTORY
BUY UNITED STATES
BONDS and STAMPS

Anchorage Daily Times
"READ BY ALASKANS EVERYWHERE"

SERVE IN SILENCE
Do Not Reveal
Military Information

TWENTY-SIXTH YEAR

ANCHORAGE, ALASKA, MONDAY, JUNE 8, 1942

PRICE TEN CENTS

NAVY ENGAGING JAPANESE IN DUTCH HARBOR AREA

PREDICT NEW ATTACKS TO 'SAVE FACE'

At Least Two Jap Carriers, 13 Other Vessels Destroyed, U.S. In Hot Pursuit Of Nipponese

PEARL HARBOR, Honolulu, June 8 (AP)—The Japanese plan for the occupation of the Hawaiian Islands has been shattered with the American forces in relentless pursuit of the crippled remnants of the enemy fleet, Admiral Chester Nimitz, commander-in-chief of the Pacific fleet, announced last night.

The Japanese appeared to be withdrawing. The contact was last with the enemy during the night, he said, but that does not mean that the pursuit has been abandoned.

Two and perhaps three Japanese aircraft carriers were destroyed by being sunk or damaged. Damage was also inflicted on at least 13 other enemy warships. All airplanes were lost on the carriers that were definitely sunk.

Admiral Nimitz said most of the planes were destroyed on one or two carriers that were damaged.

Other Jap losses included:

Three battleships damaged, one heavily.

Four cruisers damaged, two badly.

Three transports damaged.

American warships losses were reported as one destroyer sunk, one aircraft carrier hit. Casualties among personnel were light.

The gigantic battle, which rivals even that of the Coral Sea in importance, commenced with the opening attack on Midway Island last Thursday.

The admiral took the occasion to comment as to the situation as follows:

"The skill and devotion to duty of all branches of the United States armed forces have given me intense elation in rejoice in the momentous victory that is in the making. . . .

"Six months ago the Japs made their historic attack upon us. Now, the damage was heavy. It spurred the grim determination of the American people in troops sunk invariably. . . .

"Pearl Harbor has not been partially avenged. It will not be complete until the Japanese sea power is reduced to impotence. We have made substantial progress in this direction. . . ."

JAPS SHELL AUSTRALIAN CITIES FROM SUBMARINES

ALLIED HEADQUARTERS, Australia, June 8.—(AP)—Japanese submarines, slipping in close to shore under the cover of darkness, shelled Sydney and Newcastle last night in the first sea-borne attack on the Australian mainland since the start of the war.

The official announcement said the shelling caused no military damage. There was only one casualty, Edward

Hirsch, 40, a refugee who left Germany five years ago, suffered a broken leg in Sydney when shells inflicted slight damage on a block of flats.

In Newcastle there was little damage caused as far as 100 miles inland, has been ordered effective tonight. It will cover most of New South Wales.

A blackout covering the southeast coastal areas and in some cases as far as 100 miles inland, has been ordered effective tonight. It will cover most of New South Wales.

3 Given 1-A Classification

Three men were classified as 1-A by the local draft board at its meeting last night. In Class 1-A are Vance R. Jacquish, now of Selnak, Minn.; Lee Laughlin, LeRoy W. Graham.

Other classifications are: Clara L. Jacquish, E. Ghirardi, A. H. Sessions, John P. Koquaz, Alvah S. Pilkerton of Kake, Henry P. Stringer, John B. Kuechenue and Jack Kasterman, Class 111-A. Allen Strickland, Glen L. Nelson of Spokane, Kenneth L. Farley, Class 3 B. Donald H. Goodman now of New York.

Tokyo Tallies Six Months Score, Sees Japan Far Ahead

TOKYO, June 8. (AP)—Imperial headquarters reported today that 35 enemy divisions had been smashed in the six months since the attack on Pearl Harbor and that 112,000 enemy dead have been left on the battlefields of China.

The Japanese army captured 312,000, including 23,000 Americans and 61,000 British, 31,000 Dutch and 44,000 Chinese and claimed to "have shot down or damaged around 11,826 enemy planes, captured 246. The Japs put their own Army losses at 8,714 killed and 29,720 wounded, 349 planes and 31 ships lost.

Winchell Home But Plane Will Wait for Winter

RULE SUICIDE IN DEATH OF CHAS. WOOD

The body of Charles Wood 19 was found Sunday in Anchorage cemetery, and a coroner's jury this morning returned a verdict of death by a self-inflicted gun-shot wound.

Mr. Wood came to the Territory in 1898 to join the gold stampede and later lived for many years in Fairbanks. Three years ago he came to Anchorage where he bought a cabin at Ninth avenue and East G Place. He had been ill for about two years.

Little is known about him, except that two sisters in Michigan and a brother in Detroit survive him.

His body was found by two young girls whose names were not learned and who notified police.

The Anchorage Funeral Parlors have the body pending funeral arrangements.

Members of the coroner's jury were R. C. Loutzenhiser, Robert H. Wolfe, Alex Campbell, Ed Preus, Vincent S. Matretta and Luther Noey.

Warn of Artillery Practice for Week

The artillery firing over the area south and east of the Oil Well road will be continued through June 13, according to a warning issued by Fort Richardson.

The danger area is designated as follows: Starting at the junction of the Oil Well road and the Palmer highway, nine miles east; South two miles, West nine miles; North two miles to junction.

INACTIVITY NOW WOULD ADMIT JAPANESE DEFEAT

WASHINGTON, D.C., June 8. (AP)—Desperate new efforts by the Japs to break the growing might of American sea and air power in the Pacific, was predicted in informed quarters today as the only course left to the enemy which is now clearly on the defensive subsequent to the United States victory battle which started with the repulse of the huge attacking force on Midway Island last week.

Authorities said the Japs must either initiate new operations somewhere along the sweeping defense lines of Russia, Alaska or Australia, or else by inactivity admit eventual complete defeat even before the grand offensive of the United Nations starts rolling in the Pacific.

Meanwhile, the armada of battleships, aircraft carriers, and cruisers that steamed in to what appears to have been a trap at Midway, apparently had withdrawn.

Admiral Ernest King, fleet commander, declared the battle just ending might decide the course of the war in the Pacific depending on the extent of the damage inflicted on the enemy.

J. E. Ketchum Passes Away After Illness

Joseph E. Ketchum passed away at 1 A. M. Sunday after an illness of more than a year.

Mr. Ketchum came to Alaska during the first world war, homed to the Copper River & Northwestern railway by the Milwaukee railroad for the duration. He fell in love with the country and resigned from the Milwaukee and was for 15 years with the Alaska Railroad in various capacities.

He is survived by his widow, Willardie Ketchum, his father, A. D. Ketchum of Springdale, Washington; a son, Eliot J. Ketchum of Portland, Oregon; two brothers George A. of Spokane, William H. of Colville, and four sisters, Mrs. George Bloom of Hollywood, Mrs. Roy Cooney of Pasadena Park, Spokane, Mrs. Joseph LaVare of Cusick, Washington, Mrs. Harry Durkee of Chewelah, Washington.

Funeral services were set for tomorrow evening at 7 o'clock in the Anchorage Funeral Parlor's chapel. They will be conducted jointly by the Elks Lodge, of which Mr. Ketchum was a long time member, and the Christian Science church.

Fractures Hip In Truck Mishap

Miss Kathleen K. Dunlap is in Providence Hospital suffering fractures of the pelvis and several vertebrae received in a motor or accident Sunday afternoon when she was riding with

WAR BRIEFS
From Many Points

LONDON, June 8. (A)—A strong force of British bombers attacked the German city of Emden Saturday night and left many fires, the air ministry said today as the RAF's greatest offensive entered its second week. Simultaneously bombers and fighters attacked German airdromes in four European countries. The British acknowledged the loss of nine bombers and one fighter in the combined operations.

CHUNGKING, June 8. (A)—The Chinese high command announced today that the Japanese had penetrated Chuhsien and recaptured the airfield after three hand-to-hand fighting. The Chinese reported they were counter-attacking.

LONDON, June 8. (A)—Reuters said in a dispatch datelined "At the French Frontier" that Otto Abetz, German ambassador to France; acknowledged in conversations at Paris that 11,000 to 12,000 persons were killed in the RAF bombardment of Cologne and that 100,000 were ordered evacuated.

Situation Is Still Obscure

WASHINGTON, D.C., June 8. (AP)—Admiral Ernest King, fleet commander, reported today that the fleet is engaging the Japanese in the North Pacific in the region of Dutch Harbor, Alaska.

The situation around Dutch Harbor is obscure, King explained. Weather has been bad for several days. Officers in the field are required to give only a minimum amount of information to Washington.

"We have none too clear a picture of what is going on but it is going on," the admiral said.

British Urge French Evacuate Homes Along Northern Coast, Warn of 'Important Operations'

LONDON, June 8.—The British radio broadcast instructions to the French people this morning to evacuate from the broad coastal area of the Belgian and Spanish border strip which the Germans have designated a profound military zone.

"Operations" of capital importance," for the liberation of France will start in due time, the broadcast said, adding, "It has been shown on several occasions that the presence of civilian population at the scene of active operations hinders the action of troops, particularly friendly troops, in a very grave manner."

High sources said they considered the bulletin significant that it would have to stand by itself. Observers indicated their belief that the bulletin was the forerunner of further gigantic air raids on cities in Germany and occupied countries and possibly an indication that an invasion of the continent is near.

Tydings Calls For Close Check On Deferments

WASHINGTON, D.C., June 8. (AP)—Chairman Tydings (D., Md.), of a special Senate committee, today recommended that the question of deferments given thousands of young male employes of the government, be checked and reexamine to consider the question of draft deferment because of federal employment.

CAN'T BLAME 'EM

ALLENTOWN, Pa., June 8. (AP)—An scheduled baseball game between Allentown and Lancaster in 1843 was postponed when six spectators were killed.

Fix Bail At $5,000

Bail of $5,000 was set Saturday by District Judge Simon Hellenthal for Ben J. Moloch whose second trial on a charge of first degree murder is to be heard in the fall term of court. Moloch is charged with killing his brother-in-law, Albert W. son.

TO UNALASKA

Thomas H. Downes, San City Clerk Tom Downes, has been appointed manager at the Northern Commercial Company warehouse at Unalaska. Mrs. Downes and their small son, Kelly, will probably accompany him.

MIDWAY SHELLACKING LEAVES JAPS WITH A HOBSON'S CHOICE, IS BELIEF

WASHINGTON, D.C., June 8.—On the heels of the crumpling Japanese fleet in the Midway area today, two alternatives were available for the crumpled Japanese fleet in the Midway area today...

CHAPTER IX

1183

Carl Edward Creamer, 21, was a gunner on a Navy PBY piloted by Lieutenant (j.g.) Jean Cusick sub-hunting out of Umnak Island when it was shot down June 3, 1942. Creamer, Joe Brown and Ensign Wylie Hunt were the only survivors. They were picked up by a Japanese cruiser (*Takao*). Eventually they were taken to Japan where they remained in a POW camp for the rest of the war. Brown wrote of their prison experience in a privately published book *We Stole To Live*. Following his imprisonment, Creamer wrote about his POW experience, taking up his story where Brown's left off.

This is the number of days I was confined as a Japanese prisoner of war. It also represents the number of dollars I received from Uncle Sam for food during those days. My story begins September 16, 1942, picking up where Joe Brown left me in his book *We Stole To Live*.

Joe had already left the POW camp at Ofuna for Zentsuji. Ensign [Wylie M.] Hunt was still in the Ofuna camp. Mr. Hunt went to Zentsuji later. Our stay at Ofuna was rough and many times amusing. Later years became very interesting, but no less rough.

The years were interesting in the fact that American pilots kept us on our toes all the time. They [the American pilots] were very good at what they were trying to hit. I know because I spent many days and nights watching them during my three years of confinement. Their aim was so good, we were bombed out of three different camps. I became what might be called a "traveling prisoner of war."

On September, 16, 1942, it was my time to leave Ofuna. I was in a group of five Americans, two Englishmen and two Canadians. They [the Japanese] took us to the Yokohama baseball stadium. That same day, 200 Englishmen arrived from Hong Kong. There were also Americans from Kiska, Alaska there. Later, Americans who had been on the Death March in the Philippines arrived. About 250 men called the ball stadium home. Not long after, five civilians from Wake came after Japan had captured that island. [The civilians] were in very poor condition.

We worked in many different places while at the stadium. We worked as stevedores unloading salt from the barges. Many worked in the Yokohama shipyard. The place I liked best was the peanut oil factory. Prisoners who were around peanut oil knew it was very good on rice. I did not steal the oil, but many people were happy to help me take care of the oil that followed me home!

I helped many people stay healthy during our stay. I ate peanuts during the days at work. I guess that is one of the reasons I stayed healthy. The five civilians had beri-beri, and that is where a lot of the oil went. The stadium was not a bad place to be if you could call any place good.

In February 1943, the Japanese sent 38 men to Camp #5. I was one of the 38 selected. Of the 38, there were 11 Americans and we stayed together for the rest of our confinement. [These men are listed at the end of this account.] The other 27 were English. Some of the Englishmen died during the next two-and-one-half years. All of the Americans survived. It took us over an hour to walk to this new camp. When we arrived, we found that it was a Canadian camp. They had been captured at Singapore and brought to Japan to work in the shipyard. We went to work at Shibawa Engineering Works. The walk to work took us an hour. We got along well, but during the winter months the snow was knee deep and kept us wet all the time.

The [Japanese] officer in charge was a baseball fan and was always wanting to play ball. He was always yelling at the Americans to come out and play ball with him. During this time, the guards would not bother us very much. Later when we had trouble with them, we would let him know, and [he] soon had them down on their knees.

There was much sickness during our stay here. Mostly it was pneumonia. About 104 Canadians died that year. I may be high on the number of deaths, but I know it was many. During all the sickness, the Canadians were unable to work, but our 38 men worked through it all except for one American who contacted pneumonia, but recovered and was back to work in a couple of weeks. I was the only American to come down with yellow jaundice. Three Canadians also had yellow jaundice. Two of them died. The other Canadian and myself were lucky. We lived to tell about it. Through all the sickness and bad weather we were subjected to at Camp #5, we still had our original 38 men.

In April 1944, it was time to travel again. We had survived almost two years in three different camps, but it was time to change camps again. I guess you could call me part of the advance camp maker. The 38 Americans left Camp #5 for Camp #11, known as the Shibawa Camp. It was built and maintained by the Shibawa Engineering Works. We still had about an hour to walk to work.

In September 1944, 99 Javanese Dutch from the island of Java arrived, and on 2 October, we greeted 50 Australians and two more Dutchmen. I do not remember where the Australians were when they were captured.

We started getting interpreters in the camp. They were sent back to Japan from America. Our first one had been a senior at UCLA, and was one of their top wrestlers. He was cruel to us and we were glad when he left. Our next was a Mr. Tuda. He was an older man and a very good opera singer. He had lived in the States for many years and was to be married to a girl who was a senior at Ohio State. He was a very well educated person. I talked to him about his stay in Florida before being sent back to Japan. We got along well during the rest of my time. I felt that he was my friend and vice versa.

During my stay at Camp #11, the sergeant who was second in command, chose me to be his cook and housekeeper. His name was Uno San. I got along very well with him and ate all the time I was cooking (if I didn't get caught). I also helped out the men when I could who needed more food. I didn't have to walk every day to the plant and back so it helped me stay healthy. So I say thanks to Sgt. Uno for myself and also for many of the men who did not know some of the things he did for them. He was not a saint, but things might have been worse had it not been for him.

Getting back to Tuda San; he said to me, "Creamer, if you think you are watched, you should see how I am being followed. They also watch my mother's house night and day where I stay."

We became friends and talked a lot when we were not in crowded quarters. Tuda came in the mornings and the first thing he would say was: "Creamer, let's go down to the restaurant for coffee and donuts. I sure do miss my morning coffee." This man saved me a lot of grief and helped me keep many of the prisoners out of trouble. At this time, we met a young boy about 10 years old. He was working at the Shibawa Engineering Works. He said, "Yank, when are we going back to the United States? These people here don't even speak English!" He had been born in New York. So not only were the prisoners of war being detained, but persons who had no reason for being there [were also held].

On November 21, 1944, we received 564 Red Cross packages for 181 men. As you can see, we had lost 10 men. The 38 men we started out with were still alive. Later we received one Red Cross package for two men.

When Christmas [1944] came, we had the day off and were issued a Red Cross package. I guess it was wonderful when you are in a place where things like that are not common day occurrences. I enjoyed that Christmas more than the other two.

About this time we started seeing planes. None of the American planes were bothering us and were bombing at a distance. One night we were about ready to doze off when we heard this lone plane flying. [It] sounded as if it would fly right over our camp. Then we heard a bomb start to scream. We all dove under our blankets to keep the glass from cutting us up if the bomb didn't kill us. The bomb hit about 30 feet beyond our hut and blew out every window in that building. Everyone jumped up to see who was dead, but no one was hurt. One person had a few scratches. He was in the benjo [toilet] when the bomb hit and it blew him out through the door. We knew it was a Japanese plane by the sound of the motor. [Creamer said no sirens were sounded to alert the camp of an attack. Thus it would be assumed the planes were Japanese. "I suppose the Japanese attacked the camp in an effort to try and get rid of us," Creamer said.]

We were getting to see more and more planes as the days went by. We would be outside our barracks in the daytime and here would come American aircraft on bombing raids. Many times, both day and night, the Japanese guards would fix their bayonets and charge at us as if they were going to kill us. Maybe they would have, but we never waited long enough to find out. Even with the guards after us, we saw many planes shot down. We saw a few men parachute out and later some in prison camps. We saw engines burned off planes and scream to the ground. We also saw a plane fly over us and take pictures. We could almost reach up and touch it.

One afternoon the sirens started their mournful sound to tell us of incoming planes. About half-a-dozen fighter planes started strafing an anti-aircraft gun which was a block from our camp. The slugs were whining all around us. We were in our small bomb shelter which would not keep any bombs from blowing us up, but did keep us from being hit by 50 caliber slugs. They kept strafing for about 20 minutes then left.

I do not know whether they got rid of the gun or not. The Japanese were very mad at us. That strafing on concrete roads really gives a person an eerie feeling. It scares the hell out of you. We found a few 50 caliber slugs in our compound after the raid was over. We had not been bombed up to now, but our peaceful living was coming to an end. We were destined to be traveling fast and far for the next few months.

This night everyone and everything was peaceful. We had no thought of being the bull's eye for the burning of many acres of Tokyo and Yokohama. Around 11 o'clock the sirens sounded the alert. Alert means planes are in the area or over Japan. The red alert had not sounded. We were supposed to get up, put on our clothes and be ready to fight fires or leave the area. Now fighting fires with a mop and a bucket does not work. When planes are dropping tons of fire bombs—no way. The bombs were exploding north of us and seemed quite some distance. We felt we could not be bothered, so we didn't finish dressing and just sat there talking about it when we realized the Yanks were dropping bombs in a circle. It seemed we were about the center of that circle. They were dropping fire bombs. Crates of them broke up as they fell. When the bombs came out of the crates they would scream on the way down. It scared the Japanese badly, and also the POW's.

You really want a fox hole to get in and cover up fast. About one mile from our camp was a rubber tire factory. A load of bombs was dropped there to start a fire, and every time it died down a little, another load was dropped to start the fire again.

At this time we put our clothes on and [were] out on the parade grounds with buckets and mops waiting to put out fires if the buildings started to burn. I never got a chance to use the fire equipment as the bombs [began] to drop all around us. As minutes went by, the noose was tightening. Our Japanese guards were starting to worry. They were bombing within a few blocks of the camp when the guards herded us out of the camp and down the road at a run. We did not even have time to get our clothes, and left without blankets or anything. They headed us to a swamp about a half mile away. The only place where bombs were not falling. When we were a block away a plane load of bombs hit the camp right where we had been standing. It was raining by this time and we had no blankets or heavy clothes to keep us warm.

We huddled together and tried to keep warm. I guess this was around 12 midnight. The planes did not leave until 5:30 a.m. We settled down and slept a couple of hours, and when the sun came up the Japanese had us ready to march. We headed out around 8:00 a.m. We marched through the burned out area where every house and business was burned to the ground. We walked about one-and-a-half hours and came to Camp #5, the Canadian camp again. All day we were very careful what we did and how we acted. The Japanese were very peeved about the bombing raid. In fact they were mad. Maybe hurt would be the right word. The Yanks had leveled Tokyo. Later on in the day, they finally got around to giving us something to eat.

We stayed at this camp a couple of weeks getting clothes and blankets replaced. Some of the men had been taken by truck to the old camp to pick up what could be used again. Not much was worth bringing back. All of our clothes and blankets were gone and all of the Red Cross packages had been burned.

After a couple of weeks, we were on the march again. Our new camp was deep in the heart of Shibawa Engineering Works about three-quarters of a mile from the front gate. Shibawa had put a fence around a building I called a barracks, a building right on the canal for a cook house, bath house and toilet. Actually the cook house was one building by itself. Then about 20 or 30 feet from there were our barracks.

On the south side of our building, was the canal which ran from Tokyo Bay to Yokohama shipyard. On the west side was part of the shipyard docking. On the east was Tokyo Bay. North between all the buildings was the exit out of the factory. So to leave the camp in case of an air raid, our only way out was three-quarters of a mile north to the gate. [It was] one-and-a-half miles west between gas tanks on the north and truck factory, shipyard and other factories on the south. That brought us to an open area. To the north of us were 15 to 20 storage tanks. We were really surrounded.

The Japanese got us settled down and we started back to work doing what we had been doing before. This was around June 1945. The barracks were divided so the guards had the east half and we had the west. The American and English lived by the partition at the center of the building. Next the Javanese, then at the west end the Australians. By this time we had lost many men through sickness and transfers. Most of our losses were the Javanese. We were down to 130 people from our original 191.

Life went on: working, sleeping and watching planes across the canal bombing the hell out of the peanut oil factory. We had not been bothered yet. We held many safety drills; all of them at night. The Japanese would rout us out of bed, muster us on the parade ground then march us about two miles until we were completely out of the industrial area to an open space. Then we would muster to see that everyone made it there. We would be there for an hour or so then march back to the camp. We would get back to bed about 3 a.m. This happened three or four times.

On July 3, 1945, we had eaten, showered and were waiting for lights out and talking about home or whatever, when an Englishman made a statement that turned out to be the truth. He said, "We are going to get the hell bombed out of us tomorrow." The conversations stopped and someone asked him why did he think that, and he said, "Tomorrow is the 4th of July. Independence Day for you Yanks, and they will level this place."

Lights went out about 9 p.m., and I believe most of us were asleep. Around 11 p.m., the siren sounded the alert. When this happens we were to put on our clothes and muster on the parade ground and be ready to leave the area. That was why we had all those safety drills. We had just started to put on our clothes when the siren changed to red alert, meaning the planes were coming in to bomb.

We jumped under our blankets so the glass would not cut us to pieces. We heard the first plane diving on us then heard them pull up, then the bomb screaming. We knew we were done. As it happened the first bomb hit the canal, the next in the compound, and the next two hit the buildings in the factory. No one was hurt by the first plane. We started putting our clothes on again. Most of the men were dressed by the time the second plane started its dive. We dove back under the blankets. We heard those bombs screaming and some yelled: "This is it, good-bye!"

That bomb hit the building right where the Australians were quartered. About one-fourth of the west end of the building was blown apart. Under this building was a reservoir about half full of water. I believe more people would have been killed except the space between the water and floor took part of the shock. As it was, at least 20 Australians were killed. Some of the Javanese Dutch were also killed. This had taken place in about 10 minutes with two planes bombing us. When the bomb hit the building, all the prisoners headed for the only door left; all prisoners who were able to walk or crawl.

As I hit that door with about 20 others, another plane was in a dive. Everyone hollered to hit the deck. All the people who were outside except one hit the deck as a bomb exploded in the compound. A piece of that bomb went right over our heads and cut one man's legs off between the knees and the thighs. That same piece of bomb fragment tore a hole in a small building about the size of a wash tub.

When the planes had gone, we jumped up and waited to see what was next. Then we took the wounded man inside. He did not live very long. We had an American doctor in our camp. He had been the doctor for Douglas MacArthur in the Philippines. He was a captain in the Army. He and some of the boys tried to do what they could for the wounded while the planes kept bombing. We were doing this in the dark, searching for people scattered all over the compound, in the water, under the roof and many other places. Some of the crew was marched out of the area and stayed until the planes had gone. The bombing continued until 5 p.m. That raid was on for about six hours.

Not all of these planes came over our camp. They were bombing about one-and-a-half miles in width from east to west, and about two miles north. Planes were bombing from the south using the canal as a landmark. We were fortunate not to have lost the entire POW camp. The Yanks were not bombing us, but the buildings about 100 yards beyond us. We just happened to be in the way. As the planes were coming in, we were trying to save as many men as we could. Each time a plane dived on us we would hit the deck until the metal and dirt quit flying and go back to work. We had found 32 men and [had] taken them back into the barracks. By noon, 12 of these men were dead. So with the 20 Australians we lost when the bomb hit, our total [loss] was 32 people. Australians and Javanese were the casualties. When it was light outside, we counted the bomb holes inside our fenced in area and there were 20 holes large enough to bury a one-and-a-half ton truck. That does not count the ones that hit the canal. We felt that 25 to 30 runs had come in directly over our barracks that night. The Yanks had lowered the boom on the shipyard, Shibawa, the truck company and a couple of other companies. I do not remember their names.

North of us many of the tanks had been destroyed. Also, around those tanks there was a POW camp. Twenty-nine Americans were killed there during the raid. We had not heard there was a camp there until after the raid. Our 11 Americans and a doctor we picked up along the way were still alive.

We stayed in this camp about three or four days to account for all the prisoners. When all the dead were identified, the Japanese made us take them across the canal to [the] Yokohama side and cremate them. I did not make the trip, but that is one job I could do without. I have no idea of the names of any of the men who made the trip across the canal.

Now the traveling prisoner is ready for a new camp. Always heading for a new camp site. Sounds like I was on a camping trip. We didn't have to march this time. I believe Shibawa provided the trucks to take us to our new camp. It was quite a ways from Shibawa and in an area that had not been bombed. The place was in an area of small hills on the south and otherwise was a residential area. In the hills was a large cave. The camp had two barracks, one on the north side of us and one on the south side for the guard quarters; also a cook house, bath house and toilet. A large parade ground [was] between the two barracks. We were a long distance from industrial area[s] so we didn't have much to do. We got lazy. [It was the] first time in three years we had that much time to ourselves.

One day a Japanese told us about many people getting killed by two huge bombs. He said that American people were very bad to kill so many people. We finally got one of the Japanese newspapers and found that two atom bombs had been dropped.

The Japanese were not really mean to us at this time, but we knew something was in the air. One morning we got up and went outside for exercise and the weather was overcast at about 1,000 feet. It was like a blanket had been thrown over us. No sunshine whatsoever. A little later we heard many aircraft overhead. We had no idea whose planes or what they were there for. No bombing or anything of that nature. We were not sure what to think.

The next day was overcast again. We could not see the planes, but they were up there really buzzing around. No bombs, no guns, and it was very disturbing not knowing what was going on. We were wondering if we were going to be blown out of another camp when the overcast lifted. We kept our mouths shut and our noses clean. Maybe that helped because this became our last camp.

About 11 a.m., we were called out for muster. The Japanese were all in their dress uniforms and swords. Some of the guards were putting a table and table cloth with a radio in the parade grounds. After muster, we were marched to the cave. One guard stayed with us, standing outside. While we were waiting to see what was going to happen, one of the Javanese Dutch said that the Japanese were getting ready to surrender. When the radio started blaring, all the Japanese came to attention. Every time something was said, they would salute and bow. Finally the speech was over. We were told to come out of the cave.

We went down to the parade ground to wait and hear what had been said over the radio. The officer in charge started saying how good the Japanese had treated us during our stay, and that now the war was over and we should be friends. Then he told us that all the guns had been removed from the camp. The weapons in camp would be swords and bayonets for our own safety.

This is when our doctor took over the camp. The Japanese gave us paint and brushes to paint PW on the roofs of our buildings. While we were painting PW, we got the idea of painting coffee, sugar and cream. The next day our sign was answered. These items were already coming in by the time we got out of bed. There must have been a daylight launch from the carriers. The fighter pilots had put the items in the cockpit. Coming low and slow, they flipped the plane upside down and here came coffee for breakfast. This went on for almost two days. We finally had to mark out coffee, cream and sugar. The compound was getting full of these items which had broken when hitting the ground, but we drank coffee all day and night. Sure was good.

Then the torpedo bombers started coming in with sea bags stuffed with food, candy newspapers, notes, clothes, smokes and whatever they could get their hands on. Each plane had four sea bags in the bomb bay. They just kept coming all day long. Then the big birds started dropping food and clothing on chutes. This landed all over the hills. For two days, we hauled packages, parcels and boxes. It looked like we were a supply depot. We had enough shoes to outfit an army. We stuffed ourselves. We made donuts and everything we could think of; pancakes with sugar syrup. You can think of Thanksgiving, and that was our thoughts.

Then came the day we had waited for for so many days and nights. We were going home. At least we were going out to the ships in Tokyo Bay. All the prisoners got cleaned up with a shave and a shower. We got all our gear tied up that we were taking with us. We mustered in the compound. We were waiting for the Japanese bus to pick us up and take us to the docks. The bus was late and everyone was just standing there talking about home and such. What should appear but a large plane marked with a red cross. This plane was flying toward the south, wiggling its wings in salute and kept on going. Such a pretty sight to see our planes without worrying if one of the bombs would be yours.

That pilot circled the plane back north of us and headed back south directly to our camp. No one had any idea what would happen in the next few minutes. Those 90+ men standing there watching came about as close to losing their lives as we did when they were dropping bombs. All at once the bomb bay doors opened and what looked like a house was a large platform with food and clothes. Those chutes were snatching boxes of canned goods and clothing off the platform. The chutes were tearing loose from the canned goods which were six or seven boxes to a chute.

We were stunned, no one could move. There was no place to run and hide. It was too late to try for the gate into the hills. All the Japanese were in their office when about six cases of canned peas went through the roof into the office where they were having tea. All of us were running around bumping into each other, dodging cartons or whatever came down. About that time, the Japanese officers came out of their building like scared rats, yelling "What's going on?" They got out in the compound just in time to see the finish of the drop. Only one person was hurt. A Red Cross medical kit hit a Javanese Dutch on the wrist and broke it. While all this was going on, one of our boys made a statement: "Well the Yanks couldn't kill us all with bombs, so they tried it with Red Cross supplies! We fooled them. We are still among the living."

The bus finally arrived. We didn't pick up the material that was dropped. We did take the medical kit. The doctor wrapped up the broken arm until we got to the ship. We arrived at the docks and what a sight to see! All those American ships anchored out there in Tokyo Bay. There were many landing crafts at the docks. We were standing there waiting for someone to tell us what to do when we heard a voice say: "Get in the damn boats, what do you need, a special invitation?" When I got in the barge I asked one of the sailors who was that doing the yelling. He said, "Aw, that was only Bull Halsey." I said, "Okay, let him holler." I was not about to say anything about my favorite sea-going sailor.

On the hospital ship we were faced with choppy waters. One time we would be looking at the deck, and the next we would be looking at the keel. It was just like in the Bering Sea when the Japanese picked us out of the water. Finally they lowered the stretchers down and one at a time we were jerked out when the barge started to drop. We finally got aboard and started to change clothes. They wanted to burn ours because of the bugs.

We stayed on the hospital ship overnight. We slept on the top deck out under the stars and with a full belly. Then this is where 12 Americans who had been through a lot of tough days and nights parted company. MacArthur and Bull Halsey got into an argument about taking the prisoners out of the camps before the armistice was signed on the battleship *Missouri.* Finally Halsey told MacArthur to do as he damned well pleased with his Army and Air Force and the Navy would take care of everyone else. And that is just what happened.

The next day I was sent with some of the others who were fit to travel; the ones who did not need hospitalization. We went over to an LST for a couple of days. Then one day we were taken to an air field in Japan and put on a plane for the United States and home.

The pilot asked if we would like to see Tokyo and Yokohama from the air. We agreed that we needed to see what was left of the area we had been bombed out of so many times. What a bare black looking place. Then we talked the pilot into flying over [Mount] Fuji.

I arrived at the Naval hospital in Oakland, California, on September 10, 1945. I went to Seattle Naval Hospital next and stayed there until February 1946. I returned to duty at Seattle Naval Air Station. I met many of the men who had been in VP 41. I stayed in the Navy until I retired in 1960. I said good-bye. Twenty years was enough for me, or so I thought. Many times since then I would have been very happy to go back.

On June 2, 1982 [at the 40th reunion], I spoke with Commander [Wylie M.] Hunt who lives in California, and Joe R. Brown who lives in Bell City, Missouri. With me living in Florida we were spread all across the United States.

I always assumed the Canadians and English were the most hardy people. But three years in confinement taught me the Americans were far superior. Eleven Americans left the Stadium Camp in February 1943, and were together until August 1945, when we went our separate ways to return to our families.

Survivors of the Bataan Death March:
Sgt. Charles L. V. Barlow, Lenox, Tennessee
Pvt. Robert M. Juarez, Saticoy, California
Pvt. Bryon Woods, Minneapolis, Minnesota
Pvt. John Pimperal, Chicago, Illinois
Pvt. Milton S. Elmore, Glenwood, Oregon
Pvt. Eugene Odor, Newport, Kentucky
Pvt. Fred Thompson, Deming, New Mexico
Cpl. Walter Higgs, Rome, Georgia

Those who participated in the invasion of Kiska, Alaska:
2nd Cl Aero Walter Winfrey, Staten Island, New York
1st Cl Seaman Mike Palmer, Prineville, Oregon

Astoria, Oregon, May 1942, a month before the attack of Dutch Harbor

June 7, 1943. POW Photo

Sitka, Alaska, 1941.
Creamer is the second from the left in the back row.

December 1945. Twin Falls, Idaho. After release from prison.

CLASS OF SERVICE

This is a full-rate Telegram or Cablegram unless its deferred character is indicated by a suitable symbol above or preceding the address.

WESTERN UNION

R. B. WHITE
PRESIDENT

NEWCOMB CARLTON
CHAIRMAN OF THE BOARD

J. C. WILLEVER
FIRST VICE-PRESIDENT

1204

SYMBOLS

| DL = Day Letter |
| NL = Night Letter |
| LC = Deferred Cable |
| NLT = Cable Night Letter |
| Ship Radiogram |

The filing time shown in the date line on telegrams and day letters is STANDARD TIME at point of origin.   Time of receipt is STANDARD TIME at point of destination

Received at

CTJC 72 Govt   WASHINGTON DC 947pm June 24 1942

Mrs Lola Creamer Hatch

Filer

The navg department deeply regrets to inform you that your son Earl
Edward Creamer aviaton Ordnance man third class US Navy is missing
following Action in the performance of his duty and in the service
of his country X the Department appreciates your great anxiety and
will furnish you further information promptly when received X To
prevent possible aid to our enemies please do not divulge the name
of his ship or station.

Rear Admiral Randall Jacobs Chief of the
Bureau fof Naval personnel

810am 25th

WAR DEPARTMENT
SERVICES OF SUPPLY
OFFICE OF THE PROVOST MARSHAL GENERAL
WASHINGTON

January 9, 1943

Mrs. Lola Creamer Hatch,
   Box 83,
      Filer, Idaho.

Dear Mrs. Hatch:

     The Provost Marshal General directs me to reply
further to your letter of December 7, 1942, in regard to
your son, Carl Edward Creamer, and to advise you that a
short wave radio broadcast from Tokyo has been intercepted
to the effect that Carl Edward Cramer is a prisoner of war
in the hands of Japan and is well.

     The War Department is unable to verify this message.

     You may attempt to communicate with Mr. Cramer
by following the instructions on the inclosed directions for
sending ordinary mail.

     If further information from any source is received
by this office in regard to Mr. Cramer, you will be advised at
once.

         Sincerely yours,

         Howard F. Bresee,
         Lt. Col., C.M.P.,
         Chief, Information Bureau.

1 Incl.
  Info. Cir.

110

SHORT WAVE LISTENING POST

G. C. GALLAGHER, 18 Delano Ave.
San Francisco, California.

Date ___ May 16, 1945 ___ Time ___ 8:30 A.M. ___

Station ___ JZI ___ Location ___ Tokyo, Japan ___ Freq. ___ 9.53 mo.

Message (Information) for you as follows:

"HELLO MOM:- I HOPE YOU ARE LISTENING TO MY BROADCAST. I AM
WELL AND HOPE YOU ALSO ARE IN GOOD HEALTH. PLEASE WRITE
OFTEN AND SEND PICTURES. DO NOT WORRY. LOVE TO ALL."

Message received over short wave radio from P.R. Creamer,
U.S.N. now interned in P.O.W. camp at Tokyo, Japan. Address
is this camp, c/o International Red Cross, Geneva.

Above heard by writer and relayed with best wishes. Please acknowledge. V...—
Yours truly, G. C. Gallagher

In reply address not the signer of this
letter, but Bureau of Naval Personnel,
Navy Department, Washington, D. C.
Refer to No. P-2225-JT

368 50 81

NAVY DEPARTMENT

BUREAU OF NAVAL PERSONNEL

WASHINGTON, D. C.

May 29, 1943

Mrs. Lola Creamer Hatch
Filer, Idaho.

My dear Mrs. Hatch:

The Bureau is pleased to inform you that an official cablegram from the International Red Cross has been received from Tokyo, via Geneva, stating that your son, Carl Edward Creamer, Aviation Ordnanceman Third Class, United States Navy, is being held as a prisoner of war at Camp Branch No. 2, Prisoner's Camp, Tokyo, Japan.

For information concerning methods of communicating with your son and for all future inquiries concering his status as a prisoner, you may inquire of the Prisoner of War Information Bureau, Office of the Provost Marshal General, War Department, Washington, D. C., which agency informs this office that to date no arrangement has been made for repatriation of those listed in the cablegram.

In addition, the American Red Cross is endeavoring to deliver brief messages from the next of kin to internees and your local chapter of the Red Cross will be pleased to give you complete details regarding the procedure to follow.

The Navy Department fully appreciates your great anxiety and assures you it will inform you promptly of any information received concerning your son. Certainly this news, unsatisfactory as it may be, will add to your constant hope for his safe return.

Very truly yours,

RANDALL JACOBS
Rear Admiral, U. S. Navy
Chief of Naval Personnel

A. O. Jacobs
Commander, U. S. N. R.
Head of the Casualties
and Allotments Section
By direction

2706

American Ex-Prisoners of War

THE WHITE HOUSE
WASHINGTON

11 December 1945

Dear Carl Edward Creamer,

It gives me special pleasure to welcome you back to your native shores, and to express, on behalf of the people of the United States, the joy we feel at your deliverance from the hands of the enemy. It is a source of profound satisfaction that our efforts to accomplish your return have been successful.

You have fought valiantly and have suffered greatly. As your Commander in Chief, I take pride in your past achievements and express the thanks of a grateful Nation for your services in combat and your steadfastness while a prisoner of war.

May God grant you happiness and a successful future.

Harry Truman

A PPENDIX A

After the war and his release, Carl E. Creamer wrote the following for an ex-POW publication:

My introduction to PBY's, VP-41 and Husky insignia began March 1941 when I arrived at the Sandpoint Naval Air Station. Sundays are lonely days and very bad for a cocky young fellow checking into his first duty station. Only one person came to greet me: George Grath. We attended high school together in the Twin Falls, Idaho area. Monday, I found a friend, Ensign Dale Newel, direct from Portis, Kansas, my birth place.

I enjoyed my duty in Seattle. I really liked being in Alaska for three months and then back to the Seattle or Astoria [Oregon] area. I don't remember many of the sailors from VP-42, but they were about the same as VP-41.

As I look back on VP-41, I remember that it had the finest gathering of misfits ever assembled. They were like a bomb ready to explode, but very fine people; always looking out for the other person.

Not long after becoming a Skinny Wilson boy, I ran into another tall chief mechanic. I punched a hole in Ed Frolich's owned and operated PBY! Those who were near the chief know that my words are true. His words to me were: "Sailor, get needle, thread and tape and sew that hole!" I told him I didn't know how, and he told me I would learn. I did.

113

I finally made 3/c due to the efforts of Claude Shepard and Mr. Hermanson. My pay went all the way to $60. I was loaded! I was not very fond of Chief Wilson until I got to know him.

We were doing real well until December 7, 1941 rolled around. The snow was about three feet deep on the ramp at Kodiak and we were trying to get out to the magazine. We finally got there and back, but never dropped any bombs. After this we went back to Astoria, Oregon. I have many fond memories of that place, but memories have to come to an end.

After about three months we were ready for another tour in Alaska. We had finally picked up planes that we did not have to stand in freezing water to put on side mounts.

On May 24 [1942], we were on buses headed for Seattle. We boarded the USS *Gillis* for a ride to Dutch Harbor, and arrived May 29.

On June 1, 1942, I was at the barracks watching a poker game when Richard Schenck came in hollering for me to report to the ramp where a plane was waiting to take off. I still don't know who assigned me to go to Umnak. We landed there and unloaded a torpedo and some bombs. I ate that night in the plane. The next morning we departed for our sub patrol sector and then back to Dutch by afternoon.

At about dawn, we ran into a flight of Zeros. I had made coffee and had just finished passing it out. I was on the walk way behind the pilot and co-pilot with a cup of coffee in my right hand when all hell broke loose. Bullets were coming through the plane from the tail section and went sailing by me. Two of them went through my jacket sleeve spilling my coffee.

That made me real mad! Ammo went by me in the back and also the front. Fortunately I was not wounded. My life had been spared. The Zero was so lined up on us that he shot all the distance of the plane without hitting me, but two people took those shots.

Mr. Cusick [was wounded] in the right side and Morrison in the left side. I am not sure whether this was how they lost their lives or the yoke crushing into their chests on crash landing. Maybe it was both. My only injury was later on when one Zero shot into the MARK-4 float lights in the tail section.

One of our problems after landing was the rough seas. I'm not sure how high the swells were, but they looked to be 30 to 50 feet. I know that because of these swells we lost some lives and that I am very lucky to have gotten to the two man life raft. The seven man one had many holes in it from the Zero.

After it was all over there were only three people left to worry what our next phase would be. I don't remember what I was thinking at that time because everything happened so fast.

My overnight trip turned into 1183 days of confinement in a POW camp. Eventually we were picked up by a Japanese cruiser. They saved our lives because in an hour or so we would have been dead from the cold and water. That place is no place for sun bathing.

On June 27, we arrived in Japan and [were] sent to a camp called Ofuna. Little Hollywood. It was a questioning camp and a rough place to spend a few months. They wanted answers and we didn't want to give them. There were officers from the [USS] *Coral Sea* and the destroyer *Pope,* plus many other ships and flight personnel from all over the world.

(The rest of Creamer's story relates to re-acquaintance with fellow shipmates and prisoners in later years after the war.)

APPENDIX B

PBY Flying Boat

The navy PBY—patrol bomber/flying boat—was a lumbering, hard to maneuver aircraft. Yet it was a workhorse that served well when put into proper service. Among the early day PBYs was the NC-4 that flew the Atlantic in 1919, 1920s and 1930s. Among the builders of the early PBY were Curtis, Sikorsky, Douglas, Martin and Consolidated.

In a 10-year period, nearly 4,000 PBYs were built in the U.S. and Canada.

PBY pilots were trained at the Naval Flight School in Pensacola, Florida. The aircraft's crewmen and technicians learned their jobs through OJT—On the Job Training. Some trained in Seattle.

The PBY-5 was the latest model built by Consolidated Aircraft Co. in San Diego. Called the Catalina, the aircraft was a hull-type seaplane with a single parasol wing and retractable wingtip floats. It had two engines.

A flight engineer station was housed where the strut connected to the hull. In the nose, a bombadier and a .30 caliber machine gun were located. Behind the nose was a cockpit for two pilots. Behind the pilots were the navigator, radioman, an auxiliary power unit for electricity when the engines were not running and a two burner hot plate.

Midway were bunk compartments. Also located in the waist were retractable blisters from which two .50 caliber machine guns could be fired. A tunnel at the bottom could be opened and armed with .30 caliber machine guns. Bombs were carried under the aircraft's wing. Bomb racks could be converted to carry aerial torpedoes.

116

The summer months in the late 1930s was considered the only operation time in Alaska. During the summer, PBY squadrons rotated in Alaska.

Slow and ponderous, the PBY was reliable. It featured a strong air frame, Pratt & Whitney engines that started in any weather. Because of its facilities—galley, bunks and toilet—it was perfect for long patrols.

PBY-5A Catalina Dimensions

Wingspan	104 feet
Length	63 feet 10 inches
Height	20 feet 2 inches
Wing Area	14,000 square feet
Gross Weight	34,000 lbs.
Power Plant	R-1830-92
Horsepower	1,200
Maximum Speed	180 mph
Cruising Speed	117 mph
Ceiling	15,000 feet
Range	2,550 miles

PBY-5A

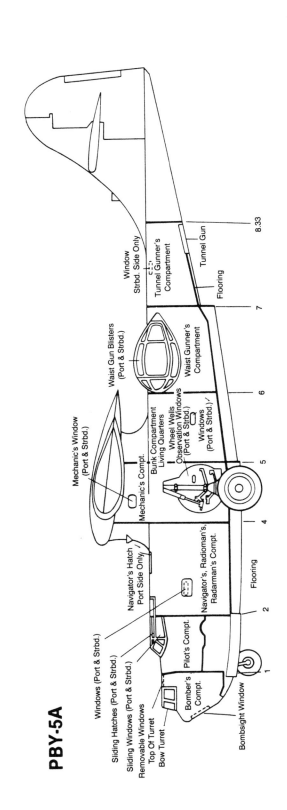

Windows (Port & Strbd.)

Sliding Hatches (Port & Strbd.)

Sliding Windows (Port & Strbd.)

Removable Windows
Top Of Turret

Bow Turret

Bombsight Window

Navigator's Hatch
Port Side Only

Mechanic's Window
(Port & Strbd.)

Mechanic's Compt.

Pilot's Compt.

Bomber's
Compt.

Navigator's, Radioman's,
Radarman's Compt.

Flooring

Bunk Compartment
Living Quarters

Wheel Wells
Observation Windows
(Port & Strbd.)

Windows
(Port & Strbd.)

Waist Gun Blisters
(Port & Strbd.)

Waist Gunner's
Compartment

Window
Strbd. Side Only

Tunnel Gunner's
Compartment

Tunnel Gun

Flooring

1   2   4   5   6   7   8.33

CATALINA SPECIFICATIONS: PBY-5A

Wingspan	104 feet
Length	63 feet 10 inches
Height	20 feet 2 inches
Wing Area	14,000 square feet
Gross Weight	34,000 pounds
Power Plant	R-1830-92
Horsepower	1,200
Maximum Speed	180 miles per hour
Cruising Speed	117 miles per hour
Ceiling	15,000 feet
Range	2,550 miles

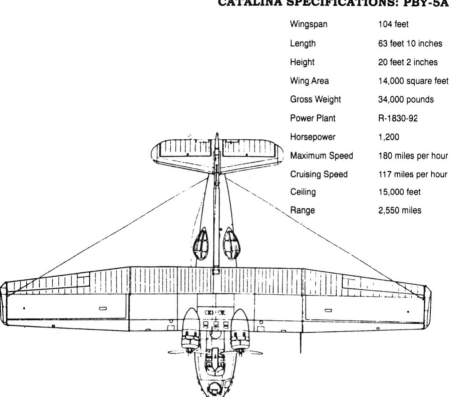

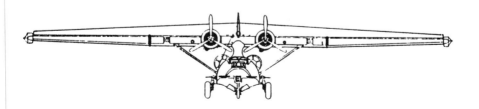

PBY-5A INTERIOR

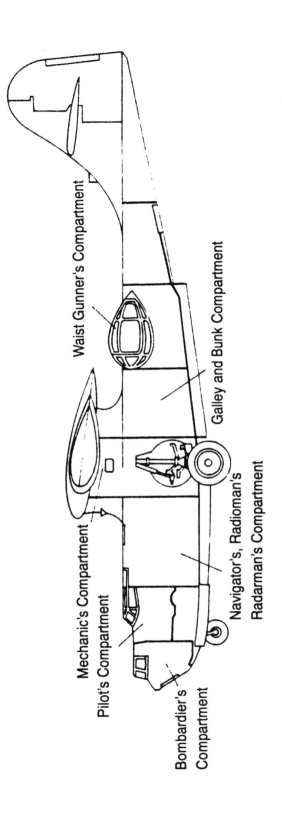

Mechanic's Compartment

Pilot's Compartment

Bombardier's Compartment

Waist Gunner's Compartment

Galley and Bunk Compartment

Navigator's, Radioman's Radarman's Compartment

APPENDIX C

The following are Japanese language copies of:

- An excerpt from the Japanese Military History of World War II.
- *Junyo* Combat Reports June 1942–January 1943.
- Naval Operations in the Aleutian Area.

戦 史 叢 書

北東方面海軍作戦

防衛庁防衛研修所

戦 史 室　著

朝 雲 新 聞 社

228

なお、附表配属艦船中、北方部隊の分は次のとおりで

してミッドウェー方面における艦隊戦闘に関する事項なので、内容を省略し各部隊の行動要領等を示した附図（挿図第十四）だけを掲げる。

第二号東光丸（給糧）、「尻矢」、帝洋丸、第二菱丸（給油）、日産丸（給油）、明石丸（給兵）、「寶戸」（病院船）

その後、珊瑚海海戦の結果、五航戦の作戦参加不可能等の状況が判明し、五月二十日第二期兵力部署発動とともに次のように一部が改正された。

北方部隊の作戦計画

聯合艦隊電令作第一五一号　二十日〇〇〇〇

北方部隊　第五艦隊司令長官は前述聯合艦隊命令に基づき五月二十日、機密北方部隊命令作第二四号をもってアリューシャン作戦に関する北方部隊命令を発令した。その要旨は次のとおりである。

第二期兵力部署トナセ（一部ツ左ノ通改ム）

(イ) 攻略部隊ヨリ第四戦隊第二小隊ヲ除キ第五戦隊（那智）ヲ加フ

軍隊区分

既述のように北方部隊指揮官は五月十日から二十日までにアリューシャン作戦に備えて左記のように軍隊区分の変更を行なっていた。

(ロ) 機動部隊
五航戦二番艦（筆者注　刑物）第十戦隊駆逐艦一隻ヲ加フ

特設巡洋艦栗田丸、浅香丸、特設砲艦神洋丸、第二日の丸特設敷設艦まがね丸を其地航空部隊に編入特設監視艇第五清洲丸を主隊に編入

(ハ) 北方部隊
第五戦隊（那智欠）五航戦二番艦、第十戦隊駆逐艦一隻ヲ除キ、第四戦隊第二小隊、富士山丸ヲ加フ

また、前述聯合艦隊兵力部署等により北方部隊に編入された艦船部隊は次のとおりである。

(二) 先遣部隊ヨリ富士山丸ヲ除ク

(ホ)（筆者略）

五月二日　第十三駆逐隊（軍清艇二十五号、同二十六号、同二

各部隊行動要領の発令　聯合艦隊は五月十二日機密聯合艦隊命令作第一四号をもって、各部隊の行動要領、作戦展則、邀撃戦法、会敵配備等を定めているが、主と

十七芸）（舞鶴鎮守府第三特別陸戦隊（以下、舞三特と略す）

五月十日　東港空支隊、特設運送船白山丸、球磨川丸、衣笠丸

五月十五日　第五気象隊

五月二十日　第二期兵力部署発動により

第四戦隊第二小隊　「摩耶、高雄」

第四航空戦隊　「龍驤、隼鷹」

第一水雷戦隊（駆逐艦三を除く）

「阿武隈」、第六駆逐隊（暁、響、雷、電）

第二十一駆逐隊（若葉、初春、子ノ日、初霜）

第七駆逐隊（潮、曙、漣）

第一潜水戦隊　「伊九潜」、第四潜水隊（伊二十五、伊二十六潜）、第二潜水隊（伊十五、伊十七、伊十九潜）

その他　第二菱丸、帝洋丸、富士山丸、富山丸、陽光丸、「室戸」

なお、陸軍北海支隊は五月二十三日集合時をもって第五艦隊司令長官の指揮下に入っている。

これら増強された部隊を加えて北方部隊の軍隊区分は次表のように定められた。(46)

1　第一軍隊区分（攻略作戦編成迄）

部隊	主隊	指揮官	兵　　力	主　要
第二機動部隊	主隊	ロ/5F	那智、2D/21dg	全作戦支援
		イ/4sf	4sf、2D/4s、7dg（帝洋丸）	AOE、AOI、AOB空襲　敵艦隊捕捉撃滅

230

附属部隊	小笠原部隊	哨戒部隊	基地航空部隊	水上機部隊	潜水部隊	AOB攻略部隊	AQ攻略部隊
	▷/7Bg	▷/22S	東港空支隊指揮官	君川丸艦長	▷/1Ss	木竹艦長	▷/1Sd
（筆者略）	（筆者略）	（筆者略）	東港空支隊（大艇×6）、神津丸、第二日の丸、第二菱丸、第五清洲丸	君川丸、汐風	1Ss	21S、21dg、俊鶻丸(-2D)、白鳳丸、13chg、舞三特（白山丸、球磨川丸）、快鳳 九、帆風、浅香丸、（栗川丸）	1Sd(-dg×3) まがね丸、陸罪北海支隊（衣笠丸）（水上機部隊）T×1
補給共ノ他	（同上）	（同上）	索敵攻撃	AOI上陸作戦協力 索敵	KL、AOE監視 敵艦隊索敵攻撃	AOB攻略	AOV破壊、AQ攻略

（註）

一　水上機部隊ハ集合地出撃ヨリ AOI 上陸完了迄 AQ 攻略部隊指揮官ノ指揮ヲ受ク

二　帝洋丸ハ集合地出撃ヨリ N＋1 日迄第二機動部隊指揮官ノ指揮ヲ受ク

二　T×1 ハ集合地出撃ヨリ N－2 日迄 AQ 攻略部隊指揮官ノ指揮ヲ受ク

四　粟田丸ハ集合地出撃ヨリ AOB 上陸完了迄 AOB 攻略部隊指揮官ノ指揮ヲ受ク

注　地名略語等ハ左記のとおりである。

AOB キスカ、AOE ダッチハーバー、AOI アダック、AQ アッツ、KL シアトル、Bg 根拠地隊

2　第二軍隊区分（攻略作戦概成後）

部隊	指揮官	兵　力	主　要
主隊	ロ/5F	那智、21S、1Sd（－dg×2）	全作戦支援
第二機動部隊	▷/4sf	4sf、2D/4S、7dg	敵艦隊捕捉撃滅
潜水部隊	▷/1Ss	1Ss	KL監視、敵艦隊捕捉攻撃

232

水上機部隊	基地航空部隊	∧OB防備部隊 海上防備部隊	∧OB防備部隊 ∧OB防備部隊	∧Q防備部隊	哨戒部隊	小笠原部隊
君川丸 艦長	東港空支隊 指揮官	13chg 司令	舞三特 司令	陸軍北海支隊 支隊長	▷/22S	▷/7Bg
君川丸、汐風	東港空支隊 (f'×6)、神津丸、第二日の丸、第二菱丸、第五清群丸	13chg 快鳳丸、俊鶻丸、白鳳丸	舞三特 (白山丸、球磨川丸)	陸軍北海支隊 (衣笠丸)	(飛省略)	(飛省略)
索敵	索敵 攻撃	∧Q ∧OB海上防備、VBN間哨戒	AOB陸上防備	∧Q、VBN、AQ陸上防備	同上	同上

附属部隊	（筆者略）	補給其ノ他

（註）

一　第二水雷戦隊区分ノ発動ハ特令ス

二　白山丸、球磨川丸及衣笠丸ハ
　　AOB及AQ
　　ニ於ケル任務終了後附属部隊ニ編入ス

注
VBN　コマンドルスキー諸島

なお、北方部隊指揮官は二十二日信電令作第一九号をもっ(54)
て第二十一駆逐隊と第六駆逐隊を互いに入れ替えている。

前記第一水隊区分による各部隊の指揮官は左記のとおりで
ある。

北方部隊指揮官　　　　　中将　細萱戊子郎　（兵51期）

第二機動部隊指揮官　　　少将　角田覚治　　（兵40期）

AQ攻略部隊指揮官　　　少将　大森仙太郎　（兵41期）

AOB攻略部隊指揮官　　大佐　大野竹二　　（兵44期）

潜水部隊指揮官　　　　　少将　山崎重暉　　（兵41期）

水上機部隊指揮官　　　　大佐　宇宿主一　　（兵44期）

其地航空部隊指揮官　　　中佐　伊東裕満　　（兵51期）

1　作戦方針

ダッチハーバー、アダック所在敵兵力を撃破し、その軍
事施設を破壊するとともにキスカ島、アッツ島を攻略確保
して、北太平洋方面からする敵の機動並びに航空進攻作戦
を阻止し、もってわが攻勢の態勢を維持するにある。これ
がため

（一）N−3日以降、母艦航空部隊をもってダッチハーバーを空
襲し、所在敵兵力を撃滅するとともに軍事施設を破壊し
て、敵兵力その他同其地利用を阻止する。
また、N−1日までにアダック及びキスカ島を空襲し、所在
敵兵力並びに軍事施設を攻撃撃破する。

（二）N日、特別海軍陸戦隊をもってキスカ島これを攻略し
確保する。同日陸軍北海支隊および艦隊臨介陸戦隊をも
ってアダックを急襲し、所在軍事施設を破壊し敵の利用を

作戦要領（挿図第十五参照）(22)

234

封ずる。

(三) アダック破壊後、陸軍北海支隊はアッツに転進してこれを攻略確保する。

(四) 潜水部隊をシアトル方面に配備する。

(ロ) 飛行艇隊をキスカ島方面に進出させる。

(ハ) 水上機母艦搭載機をもってアダック上陸作戦後アリューシャン列島以北海面を索敵させる。

(ニ) 母艦航空部隊は前二項飛行索敵に呼応し敵艦隊の撃滅に努める。

2　作戦実施要領

アリューシャン作戦において各種状況に応ずる作戦要領を左のとおり定める。

特令なければ「アリューシャン作戦第一法」により作戦する。

状　況	作　戦　種　別	作　戦　要　領
特に状況の変化ない場合	「アリューシャン作戦第一法」（AL作戦第一法）	一　北方部隊命令作戦第二四号の各項に基づき作戦する 二　集合地出発後N日若干延期せられ期日に介裕ある場合、各隊はおおむねA、B点又はC点（挿図第十五参照）付近を機宜行動し、爾後前項により作戦する
略	「AL作戦第二法」〜「同第四法」	略
アダック上陸破壊のみ取りやめる場合	「アリューシャン作戦第五法」（AL作戦第五法）	一　アッツ攻略部隊はアダック上陸破壊作戦を取りやめ、アッツ攻略のみを実施する 二　第二機動部隊によるアダック空襲破壊を実施する 三　右のほか「AL作戦第一法」により作戦する
合	略	略

AQ攻略部隊　AQ攻略部隊指揮官は五月二十三日機密攻略部隊命令作戦第一号をもって詳細な作戦計画を発令している。その概要は前述北方部隊の作戦計画でおおむね推

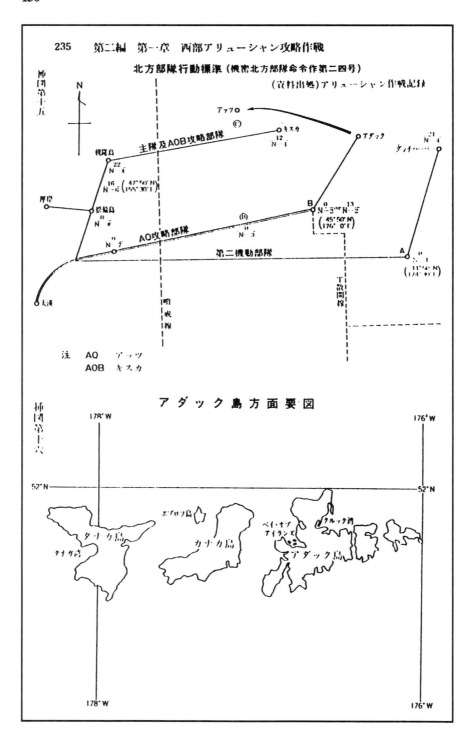

235　第二編　第一章　西部アリューシャン攻略作戦

北方部隊行動標準（機密北方部隊命令作第二四号）

（資料出処）アリューシャン作戦記録

主隊及AOB攻略部隊

AO攻略部隊

第二機動部隊

注　AQ　アッツ
　　AOB　キスカ

アダック島方面要図

238

ダッチハーバー空襲

N−3　アダック、アトカ、カナガ島攻撃

N−2　キスカ

N−1　一二〇〇 A点
　　　一五〇〇補給会合点

潜水部隊

潜水部隊指揮官は各潜水艦の任務および配備を次のとおり定めた。[22]

「伊二十五潜、伊二十六潜」五月末までにコジアク、シアトル方面を偵察、爾後シアトル方面監視

「伊十九潜」五月末までにダッチハーバー方面を偵察、爾後敵艦隊捕捉撃滅

「伊九潜、伊十五潜、伊十七潜」五月末までにキスカ、アッツ、アダック島を偵察、爾後敵艦隊の捕捉撃滅

なお、北方部隊潜水部隊と先遣部隊の作戦境界線は北緯四〇度とされていた。

北方部隊の作戦準備

集合地は陸海軍中央協定では厚岸と予定されていたが防備が不十分なことと「尻矢」の故障（既述のとおり五月十七日以後大湊で修理中）による補給上の理由から、陸奥海湾（川内湾）に変更された。

「那智」は五月十五日大湊に入港し、大湊警備府との作戦協定（後述）を行ない、五月二十六日川内湾に回航、二十七日には各級指揮官を参集して最終の打ち合わせを実施して作戦準備を完了している。[12]

各部隊は大湊または川内湾で合同しており、第二機動部隊以外は順調に作戦準備を完了し、アッツ攻略部隊およびキスカ攻略部隊は川内湾において上陸演習を実施している。若干の部隊について状況を記述する。

第二機動部隊　同部隊の作戦準備について四航戦先任参謀小田切政徳中佐は次のように回想している。

作戦準備で最も苦心したのは艦艇、飛行機の整備と作戦資料の収集であった。

特に「飛鷹」は竣工したばかりの初めての作戦で、このような大遠距離作戦の実施は不安なきを得なかったけれども、

「龍驤」一隻では兵力不足なので思い切って同行することにした（筆者注　「隼鷹」は五月三日艤装完了）。なお第七駆逐隊は南方から帰還後、十分な休養を得られず、大湊出撃前に合同できるかどうかという状況であった。（筆者注　第七駆逐隊は珊瑚海海戦に参加して十八日から二十三日の間に横須賀に帰着）

作戦資料については左記のとおりであった。

1　L方面の天象海象が果たして航空作戦に適するかどうか、明確に判断する資料がなく、沿岸には霧があっても洋上はまず大丈夫だろう程度に考えていた。

2　敵飛行場の所在と配備航空兵力については、軍令部から出されていた情報を集めて自分で調査したが、ダッチハーバーに小型飛行場があるぐらいで、新しい資料は全然なかった。

なお「隼鷹」にはミッドウェー攻略後、同地に進出予定の第六航空隊戦闘機一二機を搭載した。

舞鶴鎮守府第三特別陸戦隊　五月一日、舞鶴において編成され、二日には第五艦隊に編入、中旬には作戦準備を完了して白山丸および球磨川丸に乗船し、二十日および二十一日それぞれ大湊に入港して北方部隊に合同した。同隊の川襲準備について先任将校兼副官であった柿崎誠一大尉（兵65期）は次のように回想している。

編成前から司令官井上二三少佐は海兵団にあって聯合艦隊司令部等と打ち合わせ、秘密に準備を進めていた。隊員は比較的人材が集められ特に兵曹長、下士官は優秀であった。編制は、小銃三ヶ中隊、山砲隊、速射砲隊であったが、占領後は陸戦部隊と水際隊に分かれる関係上、山砲隊は二種の装備をした。

設営隊は約五〇〇名（のちに約三五〇名追送）で居住施設、倉庫の建築に当たるために、それぞれ技官（舞鶴工廠等から）がついて行った。

特別陸戦隊は白山丸に、設営隊は球磨川丸に乗船し、資材は両船に分けて搭載した。

基地航空部隊　東港空はアンダマンにおいて印度洋方面の作戦に従事していたが、支隊（飛行艇六）は五月十日北方部隊に編入され、飛行長伊東裕満中佐を指揮官として十六日までに横濱空に移動を終わった。

横濱空で川襲準備を行ない、五月二十六日までに大湊に進川、五機は六月三日、一機は七日幌延勘加能別基地に進出した。なお配属艦艇中、神津丸、第二日の丸は五

244

(イ) 大巡一、駆逐艦一入港中

(ロ) ウーマンズ湾内駆逐艦一、哨戒艇三、コジアク港内哨
戒艇二隻在泊

(ハ) 飛行艇を認めず
なお、同港は三十日午前零時シアトルの西北西七〇〇浬で
大巡らしい敵影二隻を認めている。

「伊十九潜」

一　二十七日ニコルスキー潜航偵察　陸上基地らしい施設を
認めず。

二　二十九日　ダッチハーバー潜航偵察

(ロ) イリゥリゥク湾駆逐艦二隻、特務艦または商船一隻、
小艦数隻在泊

(イ) 湾外六〇浬圏内哨戒艦艇約三隻、飛行機一機、河口哨
戒艇一隻を認む。

三　五月三十一日および六月一日ダッチハーバー偵察　湾内
外在泊艦なし。

「伊二九潜」

二十五日キスカ、アムチトカ、二十六日アダック飛行偵察
各方面とも敵艦船、航空機並びに特殊施設を認めず。

通信情報による敵情　五月下旬以降の多くの通信情報

の中から総合的なものを摘記する。

発大湊警備府参謀長[12]　六月二日

通信諜報

(イ)「コダック」方面三〜四隻　内一八巡洋艦ト判断

(ロ)「ダッチハーバー」方面三〜四　内一八有力ナル艦船

(ハ)「シトカ」方面　一

発大本營海軍部第一部長　六月二日

通信諜報共ノ他ヲ綜合セル敵情判断概ネ左ノ如シ

一　「アリューシャン」群島方面

(ハ) 最近哨戒機一箇中隊程度増勢セラレタルモノノ如シ

(ニ)(「コダック」「ダッチハーバー」各三箇中隊、「シトカ」一箇
中隊トナル)「ダッチハーバー」ヲ中心トスル哨戒機ハ
行動頻繁トナレリ　共ノ行動半径ハ的確ニ推定シ難キモ
三〇〇浬以上ニ達シアルベク　従来南方ヲ主トセルガ如
キモ最近「キスカ」方面航空気象通報ヲ行ヒ居ルニ鑑ミ
西方ニモボシ居ルモノト認メラル

(ロ) 潜水艦ニ関シテハ課知スル所ナキモ「ダッチハーバ
ー」ニ基地アリ　且最近ノ警戒振リニモ鑑ミ警戒ヲ要ス
ルモノト認ム

(ハ) 水上艦艇ニ関シテハ一潜戦潜水艦ノ偵察以上資料ナシ

二　「ミッドウェー」方面　(筆者略)

134

二　作戦経過

（付図第四参照）

第二機動部隊のダッチハーバー空襲

潜水部隊は既述のように大湊（一部は横須賀）を出撃してアリューシャン列島方面要地を偵察中であり、その他の北方部隊は第二機動部隊が五月二十五日大湊を、AQ攻略部隊が五月二十九日川内湾を（富士山丸だけ二十八日横須賀を出港し途中で合同）出撃し、AOB攻略部隊の大部は二十八日川内湾を出港、六月一日幌筵（加熊別錨地）に進出、六月二日同地を出撃していずれも計画に従ってアリューシャン列島に向かった。二十九日川内湾を出港、二日加熊別湾に進出した主隊は三日同地を出撃してキスカ島南方に向かっている。

一方、ミッドウェー

第一航空司令官
角田覚治少将

一方作戦部隊は予定どおり出撃して、主力部隊、機動部隊、攻略部隊および北方部隊支援の任務により北寄りにあった弊戒部隊とに分かれて進撃中であった。機動部隊のミッドウェー空襲は同隊の要望によりN-2日以降に改められた。従って第二機動部隊のダッチハーバー空襲が一日早く実施されることになったわけである。

六月四日の空襲　第二機動部隊は荒天と霧に悩まされながらも予定どおり進撃し、六月一日からは上空警戒をなしつつ三日二三〇〇ころダッチハーバーの南西約一八〇浬の地点において第一次攻撃隊（指揮官　飛鷹飛行隊長志賀淑雄大尉兵—62期）を発進した。攻撃隊の状況は次のとおりである。[41]（「龍驤」の攻撃隊発進位置における日出〇〇〇三、日没一六三九）

龍驤　（位置　北緯五二度五三分、西経一六八度四三分）零戦三機三日二三二〇発進（視界きわめて不良）、〇〇四〇ウナラカ島上空着、ダッチハーバーの飛行艇（炎上するに至らず）および重油タンクを銃撃して〇二四五全機帰着。

九七艦攻七機（指揮官　鮫島博一大尉兵66期）は三日二三三三〇発進、〇〇四五〜〇一三五ダッチハーバーの兵舎、介

庫群、乱信所を爆撃し〇二五〇全機帰等

九七艦攻七機（指揮官　山上正幸大尉─兵６１期）は三日二三

三〇発進、〇〇五五〜〇一一〇ダッチハーバーの介庸群、

油情群等を爆撃、四機はウナラスカ島西端でP─40四機と

交戦し〇二四五全機帰著

華鷹　零戦一三機（指揮官─志賀大尉）および九九艦爆一五機

（指揮官　阿部善次大尉─兵６４期）は、二二三五発進、合同し

て進撃中二三三七機二一機を発見、零戦二機は同飛行艇を攻

撃（繋撃するに至らず）後、「龍驤」攻撃隊に合同してグッ

チハーバー軍事施設を銃撃して〇三三五帰著、その他は二

三四七前記PBYを発見して繋墜したが、天候不良のため引き

返し〇〇四五帰著。

PBY

右のように第一次攻撃は「龍驤」攻撃隊と「華鷹」の零

戦二機が攻撃を実施しただけで、十分な戦果をあげるこ

とができなかった。なお、攻撃隊は〇二〇〇駆逐艦五隻

を発見（ウナラスカ島北西部のマクシン湾）報告している。[12]

第二機動部隊指揮官は右駆逐艦発見報告により、待機

中の第二次攻撃隊を含む使用可能機全力（水上偵察機四

機を含む）をもって駆逐艦群に対する攻撃を企図した。

「龍驤」（発進位置　北緯五一度四八分西経一六七度五二分）

の攻撃隊（零戦九機、艦攻一七機、〇六〇〇以後発進）およ

び「華鷹」の攻撃隊（零戦六機、艦爆一五機、〇五四五発進）[41]

は天候不良のため全機引き返した。

水偵四機の状況について当時の高雄飛行長小幡英郎大

尉（兵64期）は次のように回想している。

木攻撃に参加した水上機は「高雄」および「摩耶」の九五

式水偵各二機で、高雄機はP─40と空戦し一機自爆、一機は

被弾着水後、処分した。「摩耶」機は途中から引き返して無

事だった。

第二次攻撃は天候不良のため攻撃するに至らな

かったが、両次の攻撃においてP─40戦闘機と交戦した

ことから同方面に米軍の陸上機基地のあることが明らか

となった。第一日（六月四日）の空襲を終わり第二機動[12]

部隊指揮官は次のように報告している。

第二機動部隊戦闘速報

一　戦果

(イ)「ダッチハーバー」基地施設爆破、数箇所炎上

(ロ)繋墜　自三（内二不確実）　搭乗い俘虜　三

(ハ)地上銃撃　自七（炎上セズ）

二　被害

136

高雄九五水偵　未帰還（自爆ト認ム）

三　当方面天候不良ナルモ本朝再度攻撃ヲ期シ進撃中、状況
　ニヨリ AQ、AOB 攻撃ヲ行ハズ

計画では N-2 日にはアダック島方面の空襲を実施するこ
とになっていたのを、右報告のように五日もダッチハー
バーを空襲することに変更している。この理由について、
アダック島南東海面に向かう針路が荒天のため速力がで
ず、翌日の空襲予定地点への到着が困難であること、ア
ダック島方面の天候が悪化しつつあるのに対しダッチハ
ーバー方面が良好となりつつあることがあげられている
が、当時の状況について四航戦小田切先任参謀は次のよ
うに回想している。

　空襲当日ダッチハーバー付近に飛行場を発見、翌日これを
攻撃して空襲の成果を全うしようとしたが、前日の空襲で敵
有力部隊の北上やアラスカ方面からの空襲も予想され、司令
官としては非常に決心を要する問題であった。次のような考
えで再度ダッチハーバーを攻撃することにした。

　㈠　前日の戦果不徹底

　㈡　空襲を受けても雲層低く、艦上からの反撃となり、恐
　　れる必要がない

　㈢　敵水上部隊に対しては一潜戦の索敵、直衛の哨巡でな

んとか対処できるであろう

六月五日の空襲　かくして第二機動部隊はダッチハー
バーに向けて再進撃し、○六三四、○九四四各九七艦攻
二機の天候偵察機を発進、次のように第三次攻撃を実施
した。[4]

龍驤（発進位置　北緯五三度一三分西経一六九度七分）零戦六機、
九七艦攻九機（指揮官　山上正幸大尉）は一一四〇発進一二
四四飛行艇一機を発見撃墜。艦攻隊は一二五五～一三四
五ダッチハーバー軍事施設を爆撃し、一三四〇零戦隊と合
同して帰着した。零戦隊は激烈な地上砲火を受け、一機は
アクタン島（ウナラスカ島東方）ウナラ湾に不時着した。[注]

注　この零戦は搭乗員は戦死していたが、機体はほとんど損傷し
　ておらず、米軍は本国で修理して研究用に使用している。[後出]

隼鷹　零戦五機（指揮官　志賀淑雄大尉）、九九艦爆一一機
（指揮官　阿部善次大尉－零戦一機故障のため艦爆一機と共に引き
返す）は一一五〇発進、艦爆隊は一三〇〇ダッチハーバー
軍事施設および在泊艦船を爆撃し、左記のように空戦を行
ない一五三〇ころまでに帰着した。

零戦二機　ウナラスカ島南方でP-40六機と交戦し二機

137

Aircraft squadron Combat Reports June 1942–January 1943

飛行機隊戰鬪行動調書

戰鬪種別（ 　）　行動番號 17.6.4 —

實施年月日	昭和17年6月4日
任務	字一次ミッドウェー攻撃隊制空隊
指揮官	大尉 菅 波 政 隆

參加機種機數	
$f_c \times 13$	
f^d	$\times$
f^{er}	$\times$
f^{sr}	$\times$ 計13
f^b	$\times$
$f^∞$	$\times$

爆裝	
800×	
500×	
250×	
60×	
30×	
爆彈數合計	
爆彈所要計	

戰果	

効果綜合

所点

時刻	記事
2222	［×ハ］隊發進
2315	
2027	
2342	

彼我損害	
	ナシ
殺死	ナシ
重傷	ナシ
行方不明	ナシ
被弾	ナシ

飛行機隊編成調製表

武蔵 昭和17年6月4日

APPENDIX D

Japanese Zero
Technical Intelligence Report

(Writing in the *Daedalus Flyer*, Fall/Winter 1987, Admiral James S. Russell, USN (Ret.), told of study and rebuilding of the captured Zero that crash landed on Akutan Island.)

The most thorough analysis of the damage done to the Zero that I have seen was in the report of an Army Air Force Technical Intelligence team which inspected the airplane after its recovery to Dutch Harbor. They positively identified the airplane as an all metal (except flaps) Nagoya-type Zero fighter, a low wing monoplane with single seat and engine. The body was well streamlined and showed excellent construction. Flush riveting was used throughout. The plane was nearly new, being a carrier fighter plane, Model 2, put into service February 19, 1942, with serial number 4593.

The fuselage was about 23 feet long and the wings had a 40-foot spread with pronounced dihedral [The angle between an aircraft supporting surface, e.g., wing, and a horizontal transverse line.] The outboard 24 inches of each wing tip folded up for stowage. The wings were riveted solidly to the fuselage, not at all like ours. The horizontal tail surfaces had a slight negative dihedral and were placed above the center of the fuselage. The motor was made by Nakajima, a 14 cylinder, double row, air-cooled radial with a quick change power plant assembly. The fuel rating was given as 92 octane and the engine was rated at 950 horsepower.

No leak proofing, armor protection, destructor devices, IFF or similar equipment were discovered.

[After the Zero was rebuilt, flight testing began.] We found the Zero could outmaneuver most of our aircraft below 250 mph!

We were surprised at the Zero's unusually light weight. It had about two-thirds the weight of an F4F, half the weight of a P-51 and about one-third the weight of a P-47. The other side of the coin was that it had no armor, no real supercharger, no self-sealing tanks, no IFF and no big speed. But it was very stable and it did have hydraulics to raise the gear and our test pilots loved that. We were also impressed by the fact that the airplane's high performance was achieved with an engine of under 1,000 horsepower. That was the secret of its great range.

It was quickly established that the Zero's greatest weaknesses lay in its poor diving ability and in its lack of armor. The flight tests revealed as well that above 300 mph the Zero responded sluggishly to aileron control. It was also limited in altitude performance. Aware of the Zero's minutest details, we adjusted our combat tactics and word went out to our flyers with advice on dealing with Zeros such as:

- Stay at high altitude while looking.
- Don't dogfight the Zero—ever.
- Keep your speed over 300 mph in action.
- Never follow a Zero into a climb at slow speed—you'll stall out just when the Zero becomes most maneuverable.
- If a Zero is behind you, fly at max speed and do a sharp break right. (The Zero turned more sharply to the left than to the right.)

******

In their book *Zero!*, authors Jiro Hirokoshi and Masatake Okumiya wrote of the plane's importance:

"The attack on Pearl Harbor and Japan's war on the United States would have appeared even to Emperor Hirohito and his military leaders too hopeless to have begun without the fighter plane design which became the Zero."

Later in the book, Okiyama writes of the cost to Japan of losing the Akutan Zero to the Americans:

"Even as we reeled from the debacle of Midway, another event occurred far to the north which, although lacking the drama of open conflict, was no less serious. In the Aleutians, one of our Zero fighters made a forced landing and was captured almost intact by the Americans. The subsequent detailed study of the airplane revealed fully to the Americans the Zero's advantages and faults. With the airplane's every characteristic an open book to the enemy engineers, they could quickly assure their own qualitative superiority."

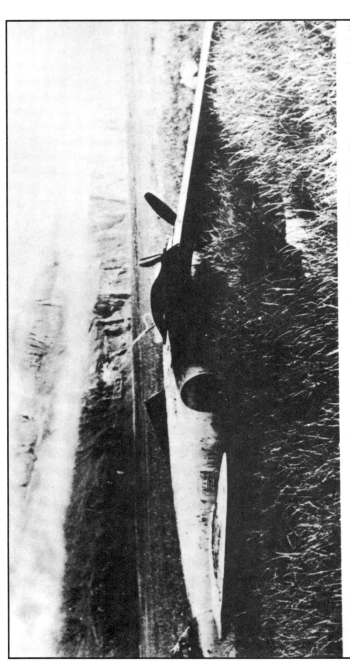

昭和17年6月5日、ダッチハーバー攻撃の帰途、アクタン島に不時着転覆した龍驤戦闘機隊古賀機──この日、古賀忠義一飛曹は2小隊2番機として出撃したが、高角砲の弾片をうけ、不時着しようとしたが着陸場所が湿地帯であったために転覆、古賀一飛曹は戦死した。写真はこの不時着機を回収に向かった米軍が撮影したもので、落下タンクが外れ、プロペラが曲がっているほかは大きな損傷は見えない。本機は零戦二一型、三菱製の第4593号機で、龍驤の第108号機であった

The Akutan Zero
U.S. Naval Historical Center photo and Maru Magazine photos

回収作業中の米軍関係隊――小宮機は右脚の小破で胴体タンクを破られており、エンジン停止のまま擱座したようとしたらしく、不時着にしかかからにプロペラが地面して動いていない。作業員は

The Akutan Zero is recovered by Americans and shipped to the U.S. for disassembly and study. Flown off the Japanese carrier *Ryujo*, it crash landed after the attack June 4, 1942. Salvaged by VP-41, it was the first Zero captured intact for flight tests.

U.S. Naval Historical Center photo and Maru Magazine photos

The "Akutan Zero" as it was dubbed. This plane came from the Japanese aircraft carrier *Ryujo*, and had crash landed June 4 after the Dutch Harbor Raid. It was the first Zero captured intact for flight tests.

U.S. Naval Historical Center photo and Maru Magazine photos

A PPENDIX E

Interrogation of Captain Sukemitsu Ito

Captain Sukemitsu Ito was a regular naval officer with 3,000 hours flying time. He had 26 years service in the Japanese Imperial Navy. At the time of his interrogation (October 9, 1942), he was a staff officer attached to the Naval Air Headquarters. From December 1941 to January 1942, he was a staff officer at the First Air Technical Arsenal in Yokosuka. From February 1942 to March 1943, he was commanding officer of the Toko Seaplane Squadron at Yokohama. From April 1943 to June 1945, he was a staff officer in the Navy Air Headquarters in Tokyo. From July 1945 to September 1945, when he was sent to his present assignment, he was the commanding officer of #724 Air Squadron, Misawa, Honshu.

Captain Ito as commanding officer of a six-plane detachment of Toko Kokutai, a Kawanashi Type 97 flying boat (Mavis) squadron, flew to Kiska from Paramushiro, landing at Kiska on June 7, the day after the initial occupation.

His detachment remained at Kiska until August 17, 1942. According to Captain Ito, from the latter part of May to the first part of June 1942, a 300 to 400 mile search was made in the direction of Kiska from Paramushiro by naval land-based attack planes (Betties). The fuel, provisions and supplies for use by the detachment were brought to Kiska on board the *Kamitsu Maru*. This ship carried 500 two-hundred liter drums of gasoline.

145

Captain Ito's group moved ashore in a camp on the northwest shore of Kiska harbor and were supported by repeated trips of the *Kamitsu Maru* between Kiska and Paramushiro. The gasoline drums were dispersed behind the seaplane beach and in the surrounding hills.

The detachment immediately engaged in reconnaissance flights searching to the east and southeast to a distance of 250-300 nautical miles. According to Captain Ito, the reconnaissance was very poor due to the prevalence of fog. Beginning on or about June 10, U.S. Navy flying boats attacked Kiska. The attacks continued for two or three days and then stopped. Captain Ito said fog probably caused the cessation of the attacks. He believed the flying boats were from Dutch Harbor.

When Captain Ito's detachment arrived in Kiska, the Japanese cruiser *Kiso* and four or five miscellaneous ships, including a few destroyers, were present. The bombing of Nazan by the flying boats occurred about mid-July. Their mission was to bomb a seaplane tender, but she was absent and the village was bombed instead.

Visual results of the bombing could not be determined due to cloud cover. During one bombing of Nazan Bay, U.S. fighters, of an unidentified type, attacked the Japanese flying boats. No damage was done to the Japanese planes except for a 50 caliber bullet hole in the tail surfaces of one plane. They escaped into the clouds.

Three planes of Captain Ito's detachment bombed a U.S. seaplane tender in Kuluk Bay, Adak, about July 20. One plane, of three outbound on a daily search, sighted the tender. When each plane had finished its sector search, they concentrated on the bombing of Kuluk Bay. Each plane carried two 250 kg. bombs. The pilots were unsure that any damage was done to the tender. One plane had a small shrapnel hole in its tail surface as a result of anti aircraft fire. The section leader of this flight was later killed at Rabaul.

While Captain Ito was based at Kiska, the Japanese seaplane tender *Kamikawa* brought in some float seaplanes.

Total losses to Captain Ito's six-plane Mavis detachment were: two operationally and three by U.S. surface gunfire on or about August 8. Of the two planes lost operationally, one disappeared in the fog between Ominato and Paramushiro; the other was weathered out [?] during a reconnaissance flight to the eastward of Kiska. This plane eventually landed in the open sea off Attu, and, although it sank, the crew was rescued by Japanese Army forces on Attu.

Replacements were received for the two planes lost operationally. Of the three planes lost due to enemy action, one sank and the other two were damaged beyond repair and were left on Kiska. Captain Ito left Kiska August 17 and returned to Japan with the remaining planes.

Captain Ito said seaplane operations from Kiska was difficult because of the weather. Searches were substantially reduced to a radius of 250-300 nautical miles due to the extreme uncertainty of weather at the base. Searches over the sea were flown "contact," while those along the island chain were flown "on top."

Ocean swells in Kiska harbor from the northeast caused considerable trouble. In spite of many close calls, no planes were damaged by rough landings in the swells. Four U.S. seaplane moorings found in the lee of North Head were of excellent quality, Captain Ito said. During reconnaissance missions, his planes navigated by dead-reckoning and celestial navigation. Although they had radio direction finders, and radio beacons were in operation on Kiska and Attu, they did not rely on radio bearings.

Captain Ito's flying boat detachment operated under orders of the commander of the Fifth Fleet, whose headquarters were at Ominato or Paramushiro. The commanding officer of No. 3 Special Naval Landing Force on Kiska was Lieutenant Commander Mukai.

APPENDIX F

From the diary of a Japanese medical officer

After the battle of Attu, pages from a diary kept by Paul Nobuo Tatsoguichi, a Japanese medical officer, were found. They reveal the final days of the struggle for Attu.

The U.S. Army learned more about Tatsoguichi from his personal effects, and further research about him. He was killed during the battle of Attu.

Tatsoguichi studied medicine at Pacific Union College from 1929 to 1932. He received his California Medical License in 1938. He was a medical missionary for the Seventh Day Adventist Church.

While in California, he met Taeko Miyake, whose parents were missionaries in Hawaii. Paul and Taeko would fall in love and marry before they returned to Japan. They had two daughters: Joy Misaka, born September 4, 1940, and Lori Mutsuko, born February 15, 1943. After the war, Taeko and her daughters came to the United States and became naturalized citizens. Both daughters attended Pacific Union College.

After the birth of his daughters, Paul was inducted into the guards. He was supposed to be given a commission in the Japanese Army, but was drafted as a medical attendant. He was suspected of having American sympathies. He also did not believe in the war.

MAY 12 — 0155

Carrier-based plane flew over, fired at it. There is also fog and the summit is clear. Evacuated to the summit. Air raids carried out frequently until 1000. Heard land noise. It is naval gun firing. Prepared battle equipment. INFORMATION [sic] — American transports, about 41, begin landing at Hokkai Miokai [it was a common practice to rename places using Japanese names]. Twenty boats landed at Massacre Bay. It seems that they are going to unload heavy equipment. DAY'S ACTIVITIES — Air raid, naval gun firing, and landing of American troops.

MAY 13 — BATTLE

The U.S. forces landed at Shiba Dai and Massacre Bay. The enemy has advanced to the bottom of Missumi Yama from Shiba Dai. Have engaged them. On the other hand, Massacre Bay is defended by only one platoon, but upon the unexpected attack, the AA machine gun cannon was destroyed and we have withdrawn. In night attack, we have captured twenty enemy rifles. There is tremendous mountain artillery gun firing. Approximately fifteen patients came to the field hospital. The field hospital is attached to the Arai Engineers Unit.

MAY 14 — BATTLE

Our two submarines from Kiska assisting us have greatly damaged two enemy ships. The enemy has advanced to the bottom of Missumi Yama. First Lt. Suyuki died by shots from a rifle. Continuous flow of wounded in the field hospital. Took refuge in the trenches during the daytime and took care of the patients during bombardment. Enemy strength must be a division. Our desperate defense is holding up well.

MAY 15 — BATTLE

Continuous flow of casualties to our field hospital caused by fierce bombardment of enemy land and naval forces. The enemy has a great number of negroes and Indians. The West arm units have withdrawn to near Shitigati Dai. In a raid I was ordered to the West arm but it was called off. Just lay down from fatigue in the barracks. Facial expression of soldiers back from the West arm is tense. They all went back to the firing line soon.

MAY 16 — BATTLE

If Shitigati Dai is occupied by the enemy, the fate of East arm is decided. So burnt documents and prepared to destroy the patients [the Japanese custom was to kill patients rather than allow them to be captured]. At the moment there was an order from Hq. of sector unit. Proceeded to Chicagof Harbor by way of Umanose, 0100 in the morning. There was an air raid so took refuge in the former field hospital cave. The guns of a Lockheed spitted fire and flew past our cave.

MAY 17 — BATTLE

At night about 1800, under cover of darkness, left the cave. The stretcher went over muddy roads and steep hills of no-man's land. No matter how far or how much he [unknown reference] went, we did not get to the pass. Was rather irritated in the fog, by the thought of getting lost. Sat down after every 20 or 30 steps. Would sleep, dream and wake up again. Same thing over again. The patient on the stretcher who does not move is frost bitten. After all the effort met sector Commander Yousaki. The path is a straight line without any width and a steep line toward Chicagof Harbor. Sitting down on the butt and lifting the feet, I slid very smoothly and changed direction with the sword. Slip in about twenty minutes. After that, arrived at Chicagof Harbor after straggling. The expended time was nine hours for all this, without leaving my patients. Opened a new field hospital. Walking is now extremely difficult from left knee rheumatism which reoccurred on the pass. The results of our navy, the submarine and special underwater craft since the fourteenth: cruisers, 3 destroyers, airborne troups [sic] and transports, 6. By favorable turn since the battle of East arm, reserves came back. Offshore of Shiba Dai, six destroyers are guarding one transport.

MAY 18 — BATTLE

The Yenegami detachment abandoned East and West arms and withdrew to Umanose. About 60 wounded came to the field hospital. I had to care for all of them myself all through the night. Heard that enemy carried out a landing in Chicagof Harbor. Everybody did combat preparations and waited. Had two grenades ready. Second Lt. Omura left for the front. Said farewell. At night, a patient came in who had engaged a friendly unit by mistake and had received a wound in the wrist. The countersign is "Isshi Hoke."

MAY 19 — BATTLE

At night there was a phone call from sector unit Hq. In some spots on the beach there are friendly float-type planes waiting. Went to Attu Village Church felt like someone's homespun blankets were scattered about. Was told to translate field order presumed to have been dropped by an enemy officer in Massacre Bay. Was ordered to evaluate a detailed map sketch which was in the possession of Capt. Robert I. Edward, Adj. of Col. Smith. Got tired and went to sleep. First Lt. Ujue is now in charge of translation.

MAY 20 — BATTLE

The hard fighting of our 303rd bn. in Massacre Bay is fierce and it is to our advantage. Have captured enemy weapons and used that to fight. Mowed down ten enemy closing in under the fog. Five of our men and one medical NCO died. Heard enemy pilots' faces can be seen around Umanose. The enemy naval gun firing near our hospital is fierce, drops about twenty meters away.

MAY 21 — BATTLE

Was strafed when amputating a patient's arm. It is the first time since moving over to Chicagof Harbor that I went in an air raid shelter. Enemy plane is a Martin. Nervousness of our C.O. is severe and has said his last word to his officers and NCO's — that he will die tomorrow. Gave all his articles away. Hasty chap this fellow. The officers on the front are doing a fine job. Everyone who heard this became desperate and things became disorderly.

MAY 22 — BATTLE

At 0600 air raid again. Strafing killed one medical man. Okayaki wounded in right thigh and fractured arm. During the night a mortar shell came awfully close.

MAY 23 — BATTLE

Seventeen friendly medium bombers destroyed a cruiser offshore. By naval gun firing, a hit was scored on the pillar of a tent for patients and the tent gave in and two died instantly. From 0200 in the morning until 1600 stayed in foxholes. The day's rations 1 go. 5 shaker [1.5 lbs.], nothing more. Officers and men alike in frost. Everybody looked around for food and stole everything they could find.

MAY 24 — BATTLE

It sleeted and was extremely cold. Stayed at Missumi Barracks alone. A great amount of shells were dropped by naval gunfire. Rocks and mud fell all over the roof, it fell down. In a foxhole about 50 yds. away each — Hayasaka, a medical man, died instantly by a piece of shrapnel through the heart.

MAY 25 — BATTLE

Naval gun firing, aerial bombardment, trench warfare, the worst is yet to come. The enemy is constructing a position. Bn. Commander died at Umanose. They cannot accommodate their patients. It has been said that at Massacre Bay district, the road coming through sector unit headquarters is isolated. Am suffering from diarrhea and feel dizzy.

MAY 26 — BATTLE

By naval gun firing it felt like the Misaumi barracks blew up and things lit up tremendously. Consciousness becomes vague. One tent burned down by a hit from incendiary bombs. Strafing planes hit the next room, two hits from a .50 calibre shell, one stopped in the ceiling and the other penetrated. My room is an awful mess from sand and pebbles that have come from the roof. First Lt. from medical corps is wounded. There was a ceremony to grant the Imperial Edict. The last line of Umanose was broken through. No hope for reinforcements. Will die for the cause of Imperial Edict.

MAY 27 — BATTLE

Diarrhea continues, pain is severe. Took everything from pills, opium, morphine, then slept pretty well. Strafing by planes. There is less than a thousand left of more than 2000 troops. Wounded from coast defense unit field hospital Hq. field post office here. The rest are on the front line.

MAY 28 — BATTLE

The remaining ration is only for two days. Our artillery has been completely destroyed. There is sound of trench mortar, also of AA gun. The company on the bottom of Attu Fuji has been completely annihilated except one. Rations for about two days. I wonder if Commander Yenegami and some of his men are still living. Other companies have been completely annihilated except one or two. Three hundred and third battalion has been defeated. Yenegami is still holding Umanose. Continuous cases of suicide. Half of the sector

Unit Hq. was blown up. Heard that they gave 400 shots of morphine to seriously wounded and killed them. Ate half fried thistle. It is the first time I have eaten something fresh in six months. It is a delicacy. Order from the Sector Commander to move the field hospital to the island, but was called off.

MAY 29 — BATTLE

Today at 2000 we assembled in front of Hq. The field hospital took part too. The last assault is to be carried out. All the patients in the hospital were made to commit suicide. Only 33 years of living and I am to die here, I have no regrets. A Banzie to emperor. I am grateful that I have kept the peace of my soul which Enkist bestowed upon me. Goodbye Taeko, my beloved wife, Misaka who just became four years old will grow up unhindered. I feel sorry for you Mutsuko, born February of this year and never will see your father. Well, be good Matsue [brother], goodbye. The number participating in this attack is almost a thousand to take enemy artillery position. It seems like the enemy is expecting an all-out attack tomorrow.

APPENDIX G

Vice Admiral Hiroichi Samejima wrote this article for the author. It is a compilation of three articles that were originally published November 1980–January 1981 in *Japanese Maritime Self Defense Force* magazine.

I participated in the air raid against Dutch Harbor on June 4–5, 1942 [Japanese time].

The main purpose of the Aleutian operations by Japanese task forces was to defend the Japanese homeland from an attack by U.S. naval carrier task forces through the Northern Pacific Ocean, and from an attack by U.S. land based bombers using air bases in the Aleutian Islands.

The Aleutian operations also aimed to create a diversion from the Midway occupation operations which were carried out concurrently. By striking in the Aleutians, it was hoped that the U.S. Pacific Fleet could be split and the occupation of Midway accomplished.

In the Aleutian operations, it was planned that Army troops would be landed on Attu Island, and Navy troops would be landed on Kiska Island. Northern Fleet was given the mission to support the occupation troops, and also to destroy American air forces in Dutch Harbor and Adak by carrier task forces. In order to carry out the air operations against Dutch Harbor and Adak, the Second Carrier Task Force, commanded by Rear Admiral Kakuji Kakuta, was organized. (The First Carrier Task Force was engaged in the

154

mission to support the Midway operation.) The Second Carrier Task Force, consisting of two carriers, two heavy cruisers and five destroyers, left Ominato Port on May 25, 1942 for Dutch Harbor.

Soon after leaving Ominato Port, the weather became very bad. Every day the task force encountered thick fog and rough seas. The fog did not disappear even with winds of more than 30 knots, and its ceiling was only about 250 feet. Neither the carrier nor the aircraft were equipped with radar, and so the patrol flight was difficult for our pilots.

It was ordered that the air raid against Dutch Harbor should be carried out after 0000 hours of June 4 (Japan standard time [JST]) in connection with the Midway operation. The Second Carrier Task Force started its air operations by dispatching the carrier aircraft from 180 sea miles southwest of Dutch Harbor at about 2300 hours of June 3 [JST].

The attack forces of the carrier *Ryujo* were divided into two assault units. The first unit consisted of seven attack planes (Kate torpedo-bombers) and three Zero fighters, the second unit consisted of seven Kate torpedo-bombers and six Zero fighters. I commanded the first assault unit, and Lieutenant Masayuki Yamagami, skipper of the Kate squadron, was commander of the second assault unit.

The first assault unit left the carrier at about 2300 hours on June 3 for Dutch Harbor. At departure, sunrise was 0003 hours on June 4, and sunset was 1629 hours. It was not dark, the visibility was bad because of foggy weather and a low ceiling. Sea level temperature was near 0 degrees C. According to the weather report from our submarine patrolling off Dutch Harbor, the weather around Dutch Harbor was improving. We flew a low altitude formation flight.

I soon became aware my aircraft speed was falling, and I moved the throttle lever ahead little by little [to maintain air speed]. The problem was carburetor icing. Although the icing prevention lever had been on, I could not stop the icing. Other planes seemed to have the same problem, as formation flights were being disturbed. I was concerned about what I should do: go on or return to the carrier. The throttle lever almost reached full power. Suddenly, I felt a roar of the engine under full power. I knew the ice stuck at the entrance of the carburetor was blown off. I moved the throttle lever to a normal position, and was relieved that I could do my duty and attack Dutch Harbor.

After 0030 hours on June 4, the coast of Unalaska Island came in sight. It was light, and blue sky appeared as we approached. We climbed toward the blue sky until we reached an altitude of 2,000 meters. We turned toward Dutch Harbor from the southeast coast. It was clear over Dutch Harbor.

The primary mission for our unit was to attack the military airfield, destroying the airplanes and the facilities. We looked for the airfield around the Dutch Harbor area and its vicinity not covered by the clouds. We couldn't find it, so we attacked the second target, a radio station, which fortunately we found.

I divided my unit into three groups. I led the first group of four Kate torpedo-bombers attacking the radio station. The second group, of three Kate torpedo-bombers, bombed military facilities and warehouses. The third group of three escort fighters, shot the moored flying boats and oil tanks. No enemy fighters intercepted our attack.

Our attack surprised American forces in Dutch Harbor, because we encountered no anti-aircraft fire while we were looking for the airfield. Later we encountered heavy anti-aircraft fire when we attacked the radio station. I was impressed with the intense anti-aircraft fire in this northern remote island.

Fortunately we finished our attack without damage. Our rendezvous place at the western end of Unalaska Island was covered with thick clouds. We flew under the clouds and joined at the strait between Unalaska Island and neighboring Umnak Island. It was about 0245 hours on June 4 when we returned to the carrier. We knew the assault forces of the *Junyo* had returned to the carrier after they were halfway to their target with the same carburetor icing conditions.

The second *Ryujo* attack unit, which left the carrier about thirty minutes after our departure, also attacked Dutch Harbor. The Kates waited for enemy fighters near the rendezvous place. Suddenly they were attacked by four P-40 fighters. Fortunately, the Kates escaped into the clouds, and returned to the carrier safely. The existence of an airfield was evident by the attack of the P-40s. I was shocked with the report concerning the P-40 attack, because my primary mission was to find the airfield and destroy the aircraft. But neither did *Ryujo*'s second attack force find the airfield.

The task force commander made every effort to find and attack the airfield. At the same time, all available aircraft were used to attack five destroyers, *Ryujo*'s second unit found in Makushin Bay located at the northwestern part of Unalaska Bay.

Four sea planes were catapulted off our heavy cruisers. They were joined by attack forces of the *Junyo*, consisting of six Zero fighters and fifteen 99-type dive-bombers. The *Ryujo*'s attack forces, divided into two units, also took off. I was commander of the *Ryujo*'s first unit which departed at about 0600 on June 4. The second unit took off about 0615 hours. It was only six hours after the *Ryujo*'s first attack, and the weather had worsened.

Clouds were almost at sea level as we neared Unalaska Island. It was impossible to go forward in a formation, and I had to return to the carrier. The *Junyo*'s attack force, and the second unit of *Ryujo*'s attack forces also returned to the carriers because of weather conditions. Two sea planes from the cruiser *Maya* also returned. Only two sea planes from the cruiser *Takao*, which made the earliest departure, arrived at the western end of Unalaska Island and intended to go further toward Dutch Harbor. Suddenly they were attacked by P-40 fighters, and one of them was shot down. Others escaped into the clouds and returned safely to the *Takao*.

When the second attack was suspended, the task force commander changed the original plan of attacking Adak Island on June 5, to an attack on the airfield and military facilities around Dutch Harbor. Therefore, the task force stayed around the southwestern sea of Unalaska Island, waiting for improved weather conditions. The bad weather which disturbed our air raid against Dutch Harbor also gave the enemy air forces great difficulties with any air attack against the Japanese carrier task force.

Admiral [Chester W.] Nimitz, Commander-in-Chief, U.S. Pacific Fleet, who had information about a Japanese attack in the Aleutian Islands and our Midway occupation operations, dispatched a powerful surface force of cruisers, destroyers and submarines to the Aleutians. Their air force also carried out search operations.

Twelve PBYs in Dutch Harbor and eleven PBYs in Cold Bay were engaged in the search operations. Army Air Forces in this area also had been reinforced. Its disposition and strength in early June was:

Umnak Island	12	P-40s
Cold Bay	21	P-40s
	12	B-26s
	2	B-17s
Kodiak Island	5	P-39s
	17	P-40s
	5	B-17s
	2	B-24s

Our commander did not know about these aircraft. The *Junyo* assault force, which returned to the carrier on the way to Unalaska Island, found and shot down an enemy PBY patrol plane. We knew the enemy had PBYs patrolling from early in the morning, and under severe precautions. American forces in Dutch Harbor, which were attacked by Japanese air forces early on the morning of June 4, strengthened their PBY patrols, and discovered the Japanese carrier task force. However, due to rough weather, the American planes could not attack the Japanese force.

The morning of June 5 came. Still strong winds and rough seas. But the ceiling was more than 300 feet high, and visibility gradually improved. Considering the results of the previous day, all weather reconnaissance planes were dispatched. At 0634, two Kate planes commanded by Lieutenant [j.g.] Ryozo Sato left the carrier and carried out weather reconnaissance. It was reported that the weather on the way to Unalaska Island was better than the previous day. But Dutch Harbor, Makushin Bay, and the western part of Unalaska Island were still covered by thick clouds. As a result of this report, the task force commander decided to put off the departure of the attack corps for a little while, and to carry out a second weather reconnaissance by two Kate planes which departed at 0930 hours.

I was designated commander of the second weather reconnaissance mission. I had to participate in the third attack operation as one of the commanders, and was disappointed to receive orders for a weather reconnaissance mission. However, my mission was important because the dispatch of the attack planes would be concluded by my report.

At 0910, our Kate reconnaissance planes were prepared on the carrier deck. We boarded, and completed all pre flight tests. Just before take off, an enemy bomber, which looked like a B-17, emerged out of the low clouds several hundred meters ahead and dropped a bomb. For a moment, I was frightened to see the bomb dropping. But it missed hitting the carrier. The enemy bomber seemed not to have time to take accurate aim. It made a sharp turn and disappeared into the clouds after dropping the bomb. Because of the enemy bomber's raid, our departure was delayed. We left the carrier for Dutch Harbor at 0944 hours. The weather in the vicinity of our target improved. As we approached Unalaska Island, there were breaks in the clouds here and there. From these breaks, the blue sky could be seen.

I climbed over the clouds through a break. There were still more clouds at the upper part but the ceiling was very high, and the visibility was good. I thought there were no flight difficulties for a large formation of bombers and fighters. We saw a patrol PBY, but it escaped into the clouds.

We arrived at Unalaska Island, its western part still covered by clouds. But the other areas, including Dutch Harbor and Makushin Bay, were almost clear. There were no clouds to prevent our bombing. I sent my report to the task force commander, saying the weather was good enough for our attack forces to enter the Dutch Harbor and Makushin Bay areas. Then I started to search for the airfield and destroyers which had been seen in Makushin Bay the previous day. There were no destroyers in Makushin Bay and Dutch Harbor, and the airfield could not be found in the vicinity. Therefore I decided to go to the western end of Unalaska Island where P-40s attacked our Kate bombers and *Takao* sea planes the previous day.

I took the flight under the low clouds. Although we arrived at the strait near the western end of Unalaska Island, there was no P-40 attack. We could not enter inland from the strait because of the cloud cover. We left the strait between Unalaska and Umnak islands at about 1200 hours and returned to the carrier.

As soon as my report was received, attacks were launched from *Ryujo* and *Junyo*. The *Ryujo* attack forces were commanded by Lieutenant Masayuki Yamagami. It consisted of six Zero fighters and nine Kate bombers. They departed at 1140 hours. *Junyo's* attack force, of three Zero fighters and eleven 99 type dive-bombers departed at 1150 hours. In the original plan, these forces had been given the orders to attack the airfield, destroyers in Makushin Bay, and military facilities in Dutch Harbor. Because the airfield was not discovered, and the destroyers were not seen in Makushin Bay, all attack forces were ordered to attack military facilities in Dutch Harbor.

From 1225 to 1345 hours, *Ryujo* planes attacked moored PBYs, their hangar, oil tanks and warehouses. *Junyo* planes sank a large transport, and attacked oil tanks and moored PBYs. No P-40s appeared during the attack on Dutch Harbor. However, the *Junyo's* attackers fought with P-40s and shot down about ten of them, losing four dive bombers. During this battle, a Zero fighter, which chased a P-40, discovered a large airfield at the northeastern part of neighboring Umnak Island. At last the airfield which we had looked for since the day before was discovered.

It was a surprise to us that the airfield had been constructed at Umnak Island. It was located very near the western end of Unalaska Island. If there had not been low clouds in this area, we might have found it earlier. The airfield was near our rendezvous point at the western end of Unalaska Island. Thus it was natural the P-40s attacked our planes.

We thought an attack order against the airfield would be given. But our commander received an order to join the First Carrier Task Force at Midway before operations against Dutch Harbor on June 5. In the order, the commander was informed that three carriers of the First Carrier Task Force were badly damaged during the Midway operations. Therefore the attack against the airfield was not ordered. As soon as the third attack group was recovered aboard the carrier at 1526 hours, the Second Carrier Task Force moved southward toward Midway.

Thus the Dutch Harbor attack operation came to an end as a result of the battle of Midway.

BIBLIOGRAPHY

Agawa, Hiroyuki. *The Reluctant Admiral: Yamamoto and the Imperial Navy.* Translated by John Bester. Tokyo: Kodansha International, Ltd., 1979.

Cloe, John Haile. *The Aleutian Warriors: A History of the 11th Air Force & Fleet Wing 4.* Part 1. Missoula, Mont.: Anchorage Chapter-Air Force Assn. & Pictorial Histories Publishing Co., 1991.

Cohen, Stan. *The Forgotten War: A Pictorial History of World War II in Alaska and Northwest Canada.* Vol. I. Missoula, Mont.: Pictorial Histories Publishing Co., 1981.

————, *The Forgotten War: A Pictorial History of World War II in Alaska and Northwest Canada.* Vol. II. Missoula, Mont.: Pictorial Histories Publishing Co., 1988.

Creed, Roscoe. *PBY, The Catalina Flying Boat.* Annapolis, Md.: Naval Institute Press, 1985.

Dull, Paul S. *A Battle History of the Imperial Japanese Navy (1941-1945).* Annapolis, Md.: Naval Institute Press, 1978.

Ford, Corey. *Short Cut to Tokyo: The battle for the Aleutians.* New York: Charles Scribner's Sons, 1943.

Freeman, Elmer A., ADJC USN (Ret.) Patrol Squadron 42. *Those Navy Guys and Their PBY's: The Aleutian Solution,* Spokane, Wash.: Kedging Publishing Co., 1987.

160

Fuchida, Mitsuo and Masatake Okumiya. *Midway, the battle that doomed Japan: The Japanese Navy's story.* Annapolis, Md.: Naval Institute Press, 1955.

Garfield, Brian. *The Thousand-Mile War.* New York: Bantam Books, 1982.

Goldstein, Donald M. and Katherine V. Dillon. *The Williwaw War: The Arkansas National Guard in the Aleutians in World War II.* Fayetteville, Ark.: The University of Arkansas Press, 1992.

Lord, Walter. *Incredible Victory.* New York: Harper & Row, 1967.

Mills, Stephen E. *Arctic War Planes: Alaska Aviation of WWII.* New York: Bonanza Books.

Morgan, Lael, chief editor. *The Aleutians.* Alaska Geographic, vol. 7, Number 3, 1980.

Morgan, Murray C. *Bridge to Russia: Those Amazing Aleutians.* New York: E. P. Dutton & Co., Inc., 1947.

Morison, Samuel Eliot. *Aleutians, Gilberts and Marshalls, June 1942–April 1944: History of United States Naval Operations in World War II.* Vol. VII. Boston: Little, Brown & Co., 1984.

Naval Historical Center, Department of the Navy. *The Aleutians Campaign, June 1942–August 1943.* Combat Narratives No. 1,Washington, D.C., 1993.

Okumiya, Masatake and Jiro Horikoshi. *Zero!.* New York: E. P. Dutton & Co., Inc., 1956.

Potter, E. B. *Sea Power, a Naval history.* Englewood Cliffs, N.J.: Prencice-Hall, Inc., 1960.

Rigge, Simon. *War in the Outposts,* Alexandria, Va: Time-Life Books.

van der Vat, Dan. *The Pacific Campaign, World War II: The U.S.-Japanese Naval War 1941–1945.* New York: Simon & Schuster.

Articles & Shorter Pieces

Burkhart, Carol. "World War II National Historic Landmarks: The Aleutian Campaign."

Glines, C. V. "America's Forgotten Campaign." *The Retired Officer Magazine,* May 1993, pp. 42–47.

Petty, Stanton H. "He Bombed Dutch Harbor," Parts 1 & 2, *Alaska Sportsman,* April 1969, pp. 6–8, 40–46; May 1969, pp. 18–20, 53.

Pratt, Fletcher. "Campaign Beyond Glory, The Navy in the Aleutians, 1942–1943." *Harper's*, CLXXXIX, Nov. 1944, pp. 558-569.

Pratt, William V. USN (Ret.) "The Navy Dive Bomber Delivers the Knockout." *Newsweek*, vol. 20, Oct. 12, 1942, pp. 26–28.

Russell, James S. "The Aleutian Zero." *Daedalus Flyer*, Fall/Winter 1987, pp. 16–22.

U.S. Strategic Bombing Survey. "The Aleutian Campaign." *The Campaigns of the Pacific War 1939–1945.* Japanese Naval Operations, 1946, pp. 78–85.

U.S. Strategic Bombing Survey, Interrogation No. 97, Nav. No. 20, Oct. 10, 1945, Naval Analysis Division, Aleutian Campaign, carrier aircraft attack on Dutch Harbor.

I NDEX

163